Music Composition in the 21st Century

Music Composition in the 21st Century

A Practical Guide for the New Common Practice

Robert Carl

BLOOMSBURY ACADEMIC
NEW YORK · LONDON · OXFORD · NEW DELHI · SYDNEY

BLOOMSBURY ACADEMIC
Bloomsbury Publishing Inc
1385 Broadway, New York, NY 10018, USA
50 Bedford Square, London, WC1B 3DP, UK

BLOOMSBURY, BLOOMSBURY ACADEMIC and the Diana logo are trademarks
of Bloomsbury Publishing Plc

First published in the United States of America 2020

Cover design by Louise Dugdale
Cover image © gardenpics / Alamy Stock Photo

Library of Congress Cataloging-in-Publication Data:
Names: Carl, Robert, author.
Title: Music composition in the 21st century: a practical guide for the new
common practice / Robert Carl.
Description: New York: Bloomsbury Academic, 2020. | Includes bibliographical
references and index.
Identifiers: LCCN 2020003337 | ISBN 9781501357589 (hardback) |
ISBN 9781501357572 (paperback) | ISBN 9781501357602 (pdf) |
ISBN 9781501357596 (ebook)
Subjects: LCSH: Composition (Music)–History–20th century. | Composition
(Music)–History–21st century. | Composition (Music)–Instruction and study.
Classification: LCC ML430 .C37 2020 | DDC 781.309/05–dc23
LC record available at https://lccn.loc.gov/2020003337

ISBN: HB: 978-1-5013-5758-9
PB: 978-1-5013-5757-2
ePDF: 978-1-5013-5760-2
eBook: 978-1-5013-5759-6

Typeset by Deanta Global Publishing Services, Chennai, India

To find out more about our authors and books visit www.bloomsbury.com
and sign up for our newsletters.

To those peer-composers who have been friends now for decades, with whom I have always felt I could share work and ideas in a spirit of support, open criticism, and healthy rivalry. You know who you are.

Contents

Preface

Thoughts to the reader on how to use this book, and . . .
A few needling questions (that I suspect you are thinking)

If you now have opened this book, it already has marked you as a very particular type of person. You are most likely a musician. Perhaps you are a performer specializing in newer music, or are curious about the music that many of your friends and peers are playing. Perhaps you are an artist in another field, you encounter music all the time, but you want to explore things that satisfy your aesthetic curiosity in a way mass-produced pop can't. You may have even heard "classical" pieces by living composers that speak to you in a way you didn't imagine, for example, Reich, Pärt, and Anderson. You might even be a cultural omnivore who wants to understand fields outside your comfort zone (and if so, bless you, and arrange to be cloned).

But most likely you are a composer, and you are also probably a younger one. You may have this text as an assigned supplement to a course in composition, contemporary repertoire, or twenty-first-century techniques. You may have been given it by a teacher, mentor, or family member who thinks it might speak to you (or perhaps you are instead that relative to whom your *own* younger composer has given it, hoping to explain this mysterious practice). You may be just starting out, or you may be well on your way. In any of these cases, I think it will have something new to show you, a perspective you may not have anticipated, and a challenge to your thinking about this vast, disorderly, constantly changing, and often perplexing field. If it has any ultimate benefit, I hope it will start to create connections between personalities, practices, and ideas that may have seemed to you an irreconcilable jumble.

I *wish* I could be writing for a more general audience, one that's curious and keeps abreast of the major players and issues in the field. Such an audience seems to exist for the visual arts, certainly for film, less so for literature and drama, even less for poetry (though still real). Music that is not a "commercial" product, however, is low on the totem pole. People who otherwise are highly educated and consider themselves cultured have very little time or interest for music that doesn't make it through the strainer of media promotion. If you keep reading, you'll see that this is *not* a rant against popular music; in fact I see within it an emerging reaffirmation of the musical values I advocate. But a knee-jerk reaction to *any* music with the slightest degree of abstraction, that labels it as "cerebral/heartless/ugly," seems to be all too common. Ultimately, let's be honest—I'm writing both a defense of and a prediction about what has been called "classical music," the music I live within the most. On the one hand, what could be more passé? But on the other, I also believe that a framework for the conception and propagation of this music "we dare not name" is becoming more broad and inclusive every day. You'll get a taste of this thinking in the following chapters.

And so while I've written this so that a "lay" listener might understand just about everything here, it will likely be most useful for younger musicians (though peers and elders are always welcome). Anything I say will be up to them to take apart, accept, or reject. Maybe I'll end up laughable in their eyes (and ears), but I'm willing to take that risk. I don't want to be the creepy old guy who's hanging out with the young at the party while they tactfully cast about for a way to avoid him. But I care for them all the same. Frankly they—you!—are so courageous, the times are so utterly inhospitable to you (we'll get into that too), that you deserve to be honored with some frank talk and free advice. And because I love what we all do so much, I can only hope that some of my insights might advance the cause, beyond whatever I may be able to accomplish in my own art or career.

And, just so I don't start to seem too solicitous of the approval of the young, I also want to figure this out for myself. The pleasure of discovery and connection in this sort of inquiry feels very similar to composition itself. So it's also a quite selfish endeavor.

And now the *Reader* responds:

So Who Are You to Talk?

An excellent question and a challenge. I can't claim to be the most successful composer around, I'm known in the field, but certainly less than many bigger names, even of my generation. So why do I think I might have something worthwhile to tell you? I'd like to think it comes from my belief in the value of my experiences and the nature of my mind.

For the first, as I reach the midpoint of my seventh decade (a fact that my body and spirit can't comprehend, as it seems I've just started my life in earnest), I find I have an unusually wide range of musical personae. Primarily I am a composer, and that informs everything I will write in this book. I know what it's like to put notes together in a convincing manner, and by now I am deeply involved in the creation of a practice I find comprehensive, imaginative, expressive. For me, it has "globality." But this is something I will explore more fully later; near the end of these chapters I'll tip my hand as to who I am as a creative being in terms of my practice (from basic technique to overarching aesthetic), and how it has influenced these chapters should become apparent. Till then, who I am creatively can come out slowly, elliptically, tangentially. You can always google me and listen to things online. And you can skip to the end if the suspense is too great. I feel a creative self-portrait will emerge, but only as a sort of shadow that gains more substance over time, through its interactions with the ideas that will fill these pages.

Second, I'm a critic, writer, and thinker about music. I've always been such: I've loved the free play of the mind, set loose within the domain of music, blown by its winds, moved by its tides, but also discovering a course that leads to new lands. I've traveled a lot across other cultures that excite me (Western and non-Western); I've listened to and processed an enormous amount of music; I've written a stream of criticism, articles, and books. There are only a few other composers whom I feel have taken my route and reached my level (whom I will honor and acknowledge ahead). At this point, so many concepts have come together for me that I feel they have reached a critical mass, and can actually present a coordinated intellectual structure, a framework for assessing the current state of the art. I feel the way I do when a piece is ripe. It has to come out, or I may burst.

Third, I'm a teacher. And this leads to the focus of this work. For over a quarter century now, I've been sitting in a room, one-on-one, with a young person bringing me her/his piece for commentary, criticism, counsel. And all the time I've been dispensing advice, I've been listening. And from what I've heard, I have developed a strong feel for what young composers are thinking, how they make judgments, what interests them, what matters to them. I'm peering into the world beyond my death when I converse with them, imagining a world I will never see. I have things to teach, but they do too. And from them, I have a glimmer of what's ahead.

So What Kind of Book Is This?

That's been annoying me, in fact holding me back from writing for some time. One world I live in is more scholarly, so it demands research, references, footnotes. Another is critical, intuitive, and usually focused on a particular piece, artist, or some mix thereof. *This* is something in between. It's *not* a manifesto or a rant; in fact, as you'll see if you stick with me, its open approach and inclusive attitude is hardly the basis of revolutionary fervor. Yet I believe it may form an original synthesis of ideas and trends I'm observing. It comes from several decades of listening, creative practice, teaching, and a relentless absorption of art (in all disciplines) and aesthetic theory. All of this backs up what you'll read, even though it sounds casual in the way I toss it out. There won't be any extended analyses of pieces I reference. I'd like to think this is criticism in an elevated sense of the word, an examination of current musical practice, aesthetics, and possibilities, attempting to draw conclusions, and maybe shed some new insights. It wears its erudition lightly.[1] The form is the essay, the tone is that of a lecture, often very much off-the-cuff. Or perhaps it's more precise to say these are journalistic dispatches from the aesthetic front. Of course you'll find things to disagree with; the very nature of this text makes that inevitable and ultimately positive. This is not the final word, only what I hope is a step in the right direction. If it encourages debate and challenge, then it's serving its purpose. *It asks questions, hopefully some good ones.*

About the Subtitle: Are You Kidding?
OK. Now we're getting down to essentials. This whole book is an exploration of an idea that *does* seem preposterous. How could we have anything resembling a "common practice" when music seems to be constantly splintering into a host of niches, each in turn becoming home to a set of subniches? It's a truism of the age that in fact there is *no* common language left, everyone is on their own, and atomization is the norm. How can anyone get around that?

It depends on your framework. For example, let's begin with a term that's now been around for a few decades: postmodernism. It's been routine to describe the current era and the art made therein as "postmodern." It's one of those terms that everyone has a feel for, but which is much harder to pin down, in large part because it draws its very existence from an antecedent movement, modernism. Its "afterness" (we could call its posteriority if we wanted to get fancy) is in fact quite *reactive*, indeed it gives life to some aspects of postmodernism that are in fact reactionary. It's hard to say what postmodernism *is* or *is for* when it emerged as a movement based on what it *isn't*.

This seems like a blanket dismissal, but it isn't, and later on we will look much more closely at these issues to tease out the subtleties. For the moment, though, the concept of postmodernism, no matter what its weaknesses, nevertheless helped to clear the ground of aesthetic ideologies that had grown tired, rigid, and largely divorced from the deep trends of world culture. And as such, it opened up the field to a range of practices, aesthetics, techniques, and media so vast and diverse that they could—really for the first time in history—begin to interact, to interpenetrate, with unforeseen consequences and artistic progeny as the result. So one of the most fundamental points of this book will be that:

> There are fundamental, global forces driving the blending of musical elements that up to this point were considered totally inimical to one another. The fruit of this blending is no longer artistic products that are isolated and unrelated, each in its separate universe. Rather, they share far more in common than currently acknowledged. *The reason we don't see this is that our frame of reference is not broad enough.*

That's chutzpah, if nothing else. But you're a "classical" composer. How do you get off speaking in such comprehensive terms when you make a music that most regard as elitist, fringe, or even dying?

The answer to this is the topic of an upcoming chapter, or maybe the whole book. Can I only say for now that I don't believe the music I most cherish is dead yet and that it still has something to contribute? I'll try to give evidence of that. As a first exhibit, from my perspective in the teaching studio, I am truly amazed that a stream of young people continues to arrive, year after year. Each composer is driven to make music that so far no one else in the world has demanded, and each believes s/he must express a thing eating them alive from the inside. And even more amazingly, they seem to be coming in greater numbers than ever. A teacher of mine, George Rochberg, had a typically apocalyptic view when he mused (to me in lesson) that nature was preparing for an oncoming catastrophe, producing more artists than currently necessary, so there would be enough surviving to continue the game. And on an earthier level, a different teacher, Ralph Shapey, said that a big pile of manure was needed so that a single rose could bloom (his exact vocabulary was more colorful). They're dead now, and their music is now in the ruthless maw of historical aesthetic selection. At some point we all will be. And yet even if the individual's creative effort is essentially tragic/hopeless, I can't help but feel that the act is not futile, that each little tributary contributes to a stream coursing toward something fresh, beautiful, and *worthwhile.*

Still, How to Use This Text?

If you are alone with the book, use it as a source of constant inquiry. For all the pieces, composers, and concepts cited, check them out, use whatever research tools suit you (nowadays of course most of them online). Carry on an "auto-inquisition" of your assumptions and biases. Accept and reject whatever works for you, or not.

If you are in a class (or are a teacher using this in a class), there are chapters that easily sync with any number of topics that come up for discussion (minimalism, technology, harmony and spectralism, interactive arts, for a few examples). I can state that it's been used this way while still a prototype, in variety of places and contexts, and it always inspires lively interchange.

So in the course of this set of musings (essays, lectures, posts?) I will look at a series of questions about composition in the early twenty-first century, and the forces that any composer should confront, no matter what stance s/he chooses to take toward each in turn. Music is all about sound, but this text trades in ideas as well. And first off, we'll start with the vexing problem of even *finding a name* for the very thing we want to discuss.

Acknowledgments

These chapters were initially written while in residence at Yaddo, July 2014.

The Corporation of Yaddo is thanked for providing the ideal circumstances for their completion.

They were again revised, in response to feedback, and with interest in incorporating new information, in summer 2017 and fall 2019.

The initial inspiration for the set was a keynote lecture given on March 3, 2013, at the Westfield State (MA) New Music Festival. I am deeply grateful to Jason Schwartz and Andrew Bonacci of the Westfield faculty for inviting me and giving me this opportunity to focus my thinking on the subject.

My profound thanks to Leah Babb-Rosenthal of Bloomsbury, who as an editor has believed in this book when some did not and given it the support needed to see the light of day.

And my thanks to my wife, Karen McCoy, who has had to hear variants on all these thoughts jostling around for longer than a normal human might like.

A Note on References

The research for this text is basically a lifetime of listening and reading, and so footnotes will refer to relevant texts and recordings to be found in my library. For recordings, I have listed those available in CD format; obviously many (if not almost all) may be found online now in various databases. In a few cases, essentially classical masterpieces of the early twentieth century and basic jazz repertoire, I've not included listening recommendations because these works are so familiar (though the one exception is Ives, for a few pieces particularly germane to my argument). In addition, the notes are interspersed with various personal experiences and observations that might interrupt the flow of the core text, but which still shed light on various points.

At the conclusion there is a similarly personal and selective bibliography that cites works which have been influential on my thought and development, whether they are cited in this book or not.

All examples of my music in Chapter 9 are published by American Composers Alliance (composers.com. ©Robert Carl).

1

What's in a Name?

Every composer, once so identified, immediately is asked *the question*, "What sort of music do you write?" It always causes a moment of panic, because there are *so* many different answers. You can point toward a particular recognizable style, language, or tradition; indicate the sort of instruments you write for; reference ancestors you claim as yours; describe what you want your music to achieve with the listener, maybe place it in a sociological context. But in the end, the questioner is mostly asking, "What's your *style*?" And that demands some tough reflection. For me, as for many composers, the first answer is "classical." But that's a wholly unsatisfying response. It marks you are part of an elite, writing music fewer and fewer people have heard, even the supposedly educated audience you'd love to reach: the sort that goes regularly to contemporary art shows, reads the most discussed novels, sees the latest films. (Of course, one *does* also usually get a polite "Wow!"-like response, as much from amazement you even exist, as for the field you toil in.) "Classical" will also bring up one of two images for most folks: it's either music that apes the romantic tradition, and *without* postmodern ironic intent, or a highly dissonant, deliberately ugly, expressionist/modernist outburst, the only type of music produced by the twentieth century in their eyes (or more precisely, as they've been brainwashed to believe). And while there are always a few outliers who actually *do* write both such types of music, the vast majority of composers who are lumped under this category don't. So before we look for either a new name or how to cope with the one we're stuck with, we have to tease out some underlying issues.

The first is just what constitutes this music most people call "classical." It's impossible to try to define it in terms of a single style, since there are so many different ones that have emerged and succeeded one another through the Western tradition's centuries of development. So it may be better to start off with identifying its essential elements. What are the core constituents of this music?

First, *it is comfortable with notation.* Note carefully the phrasing: I am not saying everything is written down. "Classical" music has always had open-ended elements, such as the cadenza of a concerto. Later in the chapters I'll look more closely at the whole issue of openness, which I feel is one of the critical and defining ones of this era. But let's accept that the tradition up to this point has done an astonishing job of developing a notational practice that is flexible, practical, and universal. (Indeed, a sort of counterproof to this is the fact that so many of the mid-twentieth-century experiments to replace traditional notation have fallen by the wayside, by a sort of rigorous and practical winnowing.) It may seem unfashionably Euro- or Western-centric (and opens itself to the charge of colonialism), but the notation that was standardized by about 1700 now is used worldwide, in cultures that it never even touched until the late nineteenth century, and for a huge range of music. Part of its genius is that it's actually quite neutral, and hence easily appropriated by diverse users. At its core it shows pitch and duration, everything else is an add-on. Early on, attempts to notate non-Western music often blanched out their harmonic and melodic subtleties, but Western notation also has a capacity to grow in complexity, in response to any new musical objects it encounters. Rhythm is particularly hard to pin down, but once again, many of the great modern advances on that front are admirably suited to ethnomusicological transcription, which in turn filters into the broader practice. The great emerging challenge I see younger composers taking on ever more frequently is the precise rendering of noise and sounds beyond the normal pitched spectrum. One response to this is a growing reacquaintance with graphic notation after mid-twentieth-century experiments, but also I see a deepening effort to discover exceptionally precise strategies that mix verbal, graphic, and traditional elements. (Helmut Lachenmann seems a salient model.) In short, Western notation opens up great possibilities and vistas for any who make it part of their tool kit, and it has continued room for seemingly infinite growth.

Second, *this music privileges acoustic instruments, in particular those found in the symphony orchestra.* Again, this is just a starting point. All sorts of other instruments than the traditional strings, winds, and brass can and have entered into the concert composer's color palette over the last couple of centuries. While the saxophone—conceived in the French tradition as the natural link between woodwind and brass—has taken its time to enter its intended practice, jazz snatched it up fast and ran with it (creating an iconic sound of genius in the process). Only with time do we have an alternative tradition of composition for the instrument, ironically in the manner to which it was originally conceived, above all in the chamber medium of the saxophone quartet. In the twentieth century, percussion has become a standard part of the orchestral setup, with pitched mallet instruments, an endless array of instruments of relative pitch, and makers of noise (in the scientific sense of the word, yet another upcoming topic). And now instruments associated with rock and other popular music, such as electric guitars, synthesizers/samplers, laptops, and even turntables, are no longer unusual or shocking. The whole emergence of an endlessly mutating world of electroacoustic music is creating an ethos of hybridization whose effects we can only begin to imagine (and composers *are* imagining them all the time now).

The corollary to this point is that *the tradition tends to privilege (or at least protect) instrumental music.* Note again this does *not* mean that "classical" music doesn't include vocal music. Just the opposite—there is chanson, lied, song cycles in every possible language, and, of course, perhaps the synthetic royalty of all musical forms, opera. I only mean that this music is not slavishly beholden to the demands of the song (and short-duration song form). In most contemporary popular music, *you have to have words.* In fact, an "instrumental" is usually the kiss of death or at least of cult. The Western classical tradition has no such qualms about the abstraction of untexted music. The symphony, concerto, string quartet, sonata—all these tell stories that are real: some are actual narratives in tone poem form, but just as many, if not more, are not reducible to easily recounted narratives. (And can I add that everything I've said in this point applies to jazz as well?)

Third, *this music is conceived more often than not for a concert environment.* By that I mean it is music written first of all to be *heard, considered, and responded to* in a highly personal and often private manner, even if the audience is packed together into a hall. Again, this music can have a social function, but it does tend to be abstracted. Perhaps regrettably, people don't get up and dance at a symphony orchestra concert—the tradition has channeled *that* onto stage in the world of ballet. Though Charles Ives would object, we don't start singing along with our favorite concert pieces.[1]

And this too has a corollary: *this music tends to be written for its own sake, as an expression of the personal vision of the composer.* It can be commissioned, it can be tailored to the needs and abilities of specific performers, and it can reflect the interests of a patron, but in the end, it is the composer's passions that are on display. Anyone who decides to collaborate with her takes the gamble that the result will be something all can live with, even be proud of. But it *is* a gamble. As such—and this is its most radical aspect, something we'll be returning to as well—it is resolutely *non-commercial.*

Next, this music *is not afraid of abstraction or formal ambition.* To write a piece of half an hour, in multiple movements, for only instruments, is an accomplishment, but not unusual for a composer in this tradition. And so much of this music attempts to express something that can only come in this disembodied form; like architecture, it begins to define an intangible but still real space for contemplation. This ability to tie together sonic elements into a whole that is larger but no less powerful than a single tune is at the essence of *composition* (the Latin word *compare* simply means "to put together"). So even though a Mahler symphony may last over an hour, it is a journey we are willing to take, precisely because it needs that duration to accommodate the ideas and varying landscapes it must traverse. And lest you think that this property is a unique aspect of a specifically European legacy, listen to Ellington's *Black, Brown, and Beige,* or Mingus's *The Shoes of the Fisherman's Wife Are Some Jiveass Slippers*.[2] Here, you hear composers stretching the initial assumptions of their language to new lengths of expression, duration, and multiplicity. Or, moving farther away from classical sources, take *Sergeant Pepper* or *Tommy.* The list is potentially long if not endless.

Finally, something *transcendent* often emerges from this music. Of course, this is not always the case, and if it were, we'd quickly become exhausted by the sheer seriousness of it all. But it's not for nothing that the first great patron of European music was the Catholic Church, and in other cultures the great enduring musics have tended to emerge from their respective religions, and sacred rites. As we move further into the modern age, post-Enlightenment, this quality becomes more generalized. What was once explicitly religious may be instead more "spiritual." Or it may become more "humanistic." In its abstracted form, this visionary quality ties into what Charles Ives called "substance" as opposed to "manner." Schoenberg called it "idea" in contrast to "style." In any case we are talking about music that attempts to be a portal to something *beyond.*

These characteristics go a long way toward defining the music written today for whose name we search. I think, though, that it's worth taking a moment now to cast a glance backward, applying these criteria over music history. It may make our task easier and our ultimate goal even clearer.

The whole idea of a "canon" by now has been subjected to a heavy dose of criticism, at times vilification. There is no doubt that the Eurocentric, "classical" tradition is tainted by the exclusion of so many who wanted to enter its course, in particular non-Caucausian and female. It's been pretty much a white man's club, with a few outliers who managed to squeeze in, but whose presence is basically the exception that proves the rule. (To take just the case of female composers, post-Renaissance it seems to be Barbara Strozzi in the seventeenth century, then the nineteenth opens up to just two, Fanny Mendelssohn and Clara Schumann, who *did* already have a little bit of name recognition beyond their own efforts.) As such it's understandable how disreputable this looks now, even though happily the demographics are changing rapidly, and not a moment too soon.

So let's accept that this tradition is tainted by a legacy of prejudice and discrimination. Guilty as charged. And yet I don't want it discarded just on the basis of this limitation; there's just too much wonderful music there that we all can share, love, appreciate, and learn from, and yes, even appropriate. Both contemporary support and historical research can vastly expand the diversity of the roster. But can we possibly reclaim the tradition in a manner that's more inclusive, and yes, forgiving?

First of all, we need to take the principles outlined above and apply them across time and culture in a manner that's not been done until recently. It is important to realize that there are several traditions, both within the West and without, that have followed the practices and shared the values I've identified as belonging to "classical" music. In Asia, Japanese *gagaku*, Korean *pansori*, Tibetan chant, Beijing opera, Indian raga, Turkish *makams*, Indonesian gamelan—just to name a few—have fully evolved over centuries, rivaling in sophistication anything produced in the West. In many aspects, their sophistication is far greater: consider the microinflectional subtleties of the *makam*, the sublime pacing of *gagaku*, and the dazzling rhythmic cycles of the raga's *tala*. True, in some cases they are preserved as if in amber: *gagaku* comes to mind. But even here a new generation of both Japanese and foreign composers are again writing for this ensemble and its remarkable timbre, and the same can be said for many of the others above.

Further, musicology is developing ever more sophisticated tools to notate and explore music that may fall outside my criteria. African (especially what I'd call "precolonial") and European folk music can now be seen to have levels of sophistication that composers can only gasp at. Composers as varied as Reich and Ligeti acknowledge the cross-rhythms of African music as a critical influence. Bartók would not be Bartók without the pioneering musicological research and preservation he undertook throughout Central and Eastern Europe with

Zoltán Kodály. For those who object, yes, there will always be a certain amount of appropriation when formally trained composers approach and incorporate aspects of this music into their practice, and it will always be controversial. I can only respond that it's going to happen no matter what, and the more we become sensitized to the issue and look for ways to make the interchange as equal and respectful as possible, the better off we'll all be.

I'm not an ethnomusicologist, and I don't want to become too entangled here, as the field is supremely vast, and the point I am trying to make will always unleash an onslaught of qualifiers. What *is* clear is that we now easily see what was already evident in art history: there are several parallel world music traditions of equal worth, but also profoundly different from one another. And we are in a period when composers from every tradition are being exposed to and examining music outside their initial tradition.

This also goes for traditions that up till now were seen, even within Western practice, as being lesser or more simplistic, that is "popular" music. In some ways, America has been the great pioneer in opening up such music to a new level of critical understanding and appreciation. In my own lifetime, I've seen Tin Pan Alley be renamed The Great American Songbook, and we now acknowledge Berlin, Porter, Kern, Rodgers, and Arlen as masterful art song composers rivaling their European antecedents.[3]

Gershwin is an even more supreme example of a composer who truly bridges the gap. It is one of American music's greatest tragedies that he died so young (I think one of the greatest "what ifs" of all is what sort of music he would have been writing in the postwar era, still alive with Copland, Bernstein, Barber, even Babbitt and Carter.) Jazz, of course, is *the* great parallel American musical tradition, to the point that its influence internationally is greater than any other "sophisticated" (to take Ellington's term) homegrown musical language. And black musicians are a very special case, due to the cultural constraints under which they worked. It seems clear that from the very beginning, those such as James Reese Europe, Jelly Roll Morton, Fletcher Henderson, and the young Ellington were aware that they were writing a concert music that deserved to be considered in the same light as that being performed at Carnegie Hall; only racist attitudes and laws kept them out. In short, jazz is unquestionably a "classical" music by any standard, and this is a point so obvious and by now so frequently stated that I don't have to emphasize it further.

What *is* interesting is that many other popular American forms (and frankly, because of the incredible international dominance of the American product on global culture, we might as well say world popular music here[4]) are themselves reaching a point of sophistication and self-reflection that they too are now "classicizing." As evidence, we now cannot say with certainty exactly what sort of composer Frank Zappa *is*. (In fact, for many young composers, the point is moot. He's a master and an influence, case closed.) It is now clear that the Beatles are masters of song form to rival any in world history, and in fact their reinvention of larger song sequences via the LP album creates new ideas of musical form, in particular that of the song cycle/suite. Radiohead is not only a logical successor to the Beatles, but we have Jonny Greenwood writing some of the most challenging film scores of anyone today and organizing a concert that celebrates his admiration of the work of Penderecki. Loudon Wainwright composes opera. Tori Amos, Regina Spektor, and Esperanza Spalding can be called new lied composers, and Joni Mitchell now looks like their Schubert.

This game can go on forever, and any reader can choose her favorite case. The fact is that the level of awareness and education of more and more composers who choose a route that at least *appears* "popular" is reaching such a point that their music can't be dismissed as simplistic or unambitious. In fact it may be the most ambitious music around, trying to blend elements regarded until recently as inherently irreconcilable. How do we deal with Gabriel Kahane? We just do. I even see it emerging in "alt country" and/or "roots music." Who can be simultaneously more earthy and savvy/inventive than Tom Waits?

At this point some might object that either I'm slumming or I'm opening the gates too wide, admitting anyone who claims a level of sophistication in their work, whether deserved or not. Admitted, as in *every* discipline and tradition, there will be poseurs. But in all the cases I've just mentioned, I feel that the artists are clearly people who grew up in a certain tradition, but *wanted more*, just like composers throughout history. The so-called classical tradition, for reasons perhaps unfair, seemed too distant to them, if they were even aware of it. But they had the motivation to write music first, and foremost, *to please themselves*, and perhaps a small coterie of likeminded souls. Every composer dreams of success, even if it seems futile. Many of these composers have achieved success envied by those toiling in less "accessible" traditions. But frankly, none I've listed above, except for the Beatles, have achieved true *mass* popularity, that which is reserved for a certain sort of contemporary global entertainer, the "artist" who is often the front for a particularly gifted "producer." In fact, they're pretty much all "cult" artists, with serious followings that sustain a career, but not the sort of cosmic megacareer we associate with the superstar. And that, I think, is precisely the proof that they are composers worthy of inclusion in the discourse to come.

Did you think I'd forgotten my earlier point about historical perspective on the whole name-issue? No, I'm just working up to it. What we come down to is a plethora of traditions, across time, space, and culture, that all demand, and deserve, attention. And each of them is gaining enough historical duration, and developing mechanisms of autocriticism, that they can make judgments about the relative quality and durability of their product. So now, if we go back to the idea of something "canonic," we have to look over an exponentially broader critical plain. But trying to determine quality or "greatness" is futile, when one is dealing with apples and oranges, right? Sorry, but I think the standard is quite simple. What we need to ask is: *Is this surviving music?*

If we still want to hear a piece after its immediate circumstances have passed, then I say it's *surviving*. Of course, things come and go out of fashion historically as well. I remember the great Baroque Boom of the 1960s. The eighteenth century had been a realm for specialists, with the exception of Bach. Suddenly the *Four Seasons* was everywhere; there was even a long standing radio program of "Barococco" music. Jokes were made about NPR stations that broadcast "all Pachelbel, all the time." We don't have the same inundation of eighteenth-century music now, though it's migrated into the secure world of early music ensembles. Telemann is now more rooted in the repertoire than before, while not as important as he might have seemed a few decades back. In short, there's a natural oscillation here, and usually things start to shake down to a consensus after a while. But there *are* great surprises. Mendelssohn's "discovery" of Bach with the presentation of the St. Matthew Passion is a case of a composer being suddenly elevated from the realm of arcana to timeless significance, to unchallenged status in the company of a handful of "greats." I would maintain that despite a certain controversial aura even now, Ives is settling into the role of one of the most important composers of the twentieth century (Mahler got there just a little before him). Perhaps the greatest shock of all, an exhumation sine qua non, is Hildegard von Bingen. Remember my earlier remark about the historical dearth of women composers pre-twentieth century? Who could have imagined that an eleventh-century abbess known as much as a mystic, healer, and astute politician would turn out to be the first truly great individual composer of the Western tradition, predating Leonin and Perotin? Her music had to wait for two things: (1) the development of increasingly smart (and creative) musicology to restore the materials to their original freshness and performability and (2) the emergence of late-twentieth-century feminism (and yes, transdoctrinal spirituality), which allowed appreciation of her worldview as reflected in her art.

So now that we have some sense of what this music of historical substance is, or at least can be, we can return to the present. What is the potential contemporary equivalent of this music? What do we call it, what label gets to this essence?

There are a lot of contenders for the title. We've already seen the dangers of "classical music": the term does help to locate a creator within the markers of a particular tradition, but it comes with a lot of baggage. So perhaps the solution is to define this music in a temporal context. But then *modern* music, ironically, feels outdated, as modernism has become identified with a particular strand of twentieth-century aesthetics, and thus is more historical than ever. *Contemporary* music seems a better choice, but it is tied to the moment. What's contemporary at one instant is not the next. *New* music is more objective and has achieved far more currency, but it has the same temporal drawback as "contemporary," and also has gotten a lot of popular acceptance as the term for a particular sort of indie popular music, leaving its "classical" cousins in the dust. Indeed, at this point perhaps the best such term I've encountered is the one devised by the composer-critic Kyle Gann, "postclassical."[5] It suggests both the lineage and the distance of current work from it. For me it remains in the running.

Of course, we could avoid this problem entirely by simply defining the music based on the media it uses. One can say, "I write chamber music/songs/symphonies/operas/electronic music"—and fill in the blank with any of these. It gives an immediate sense of the soundworld to the questioner, but it doesn't really solve the problem of the *voice* in the music, the languages used by the composer, or the traditions s/he references. And what do you do when as a composer one works in almost all the domains listed above? We're almost back where we started.

So perhaps we can devise definitions based on aesthetics instead. *Experimental* music suggests freedom and adventure, but it also is very closely tied to a particular moment (postwar New York, the Cageian school) and its descendants, and while it makes up a thriving portion of the field, it is still a portion. *Avant-garde* music of course has a long and noble history, but then it *is* "historical" as terms go, since if its products are successful, then by definition they enter the mainstream and leave their original designation. Like political leftists trying to find a suitable substitute for "radical" or "liberal," *progressive* music has a nicer ring; it's more comprehensive or at least casts a wider net. But it also sounds a little middle-of-the-road and frankly doesn't account for music that assumes the "radically reactionary" standpoint of much postmodernist/neoromantic music (think Rochberg, Del Tredici, and Bolcom). The challenge of this music can be as great or greater than any that tries to reconcile traditional and experimental elements, as "progressive" suggests.

Of course, if we think in a more sociological manner, we can speak of the relation of this music to its presentation, market and public. *Concert* music has the clear implication of music that's meant above all to be *heard*, and in a particular manner, and I think it would be fine (indeed inclusive of many different styles) if most listeners didn't already associate the idea of a "concert" with the Stones in a stadium. Closely related is *absolute music*. While I'll return to the influence and implications of this term near the end, it does suggest the sort of abstraction that makes much of this type of music special. The problem, though, remains that much of what I'm examining and celebrating is *not* totally pure or abstract. So as such, "absolute" remains a subset. And *serious music* has a lot going for it, as it suggests the integrity and authenticity of approach brought to composition. The only problem is that the very name seems to preclude a sense of humor or play.[6]

So what about *non-commercial*? This doesn't mean music that is inherently unsuccessful or can't make money. Rather, its motivations come from forces that aren't *primarily* commercial, and frankly, without the careful calculation necessary in global economic practice, it's unlikely to make the sort of profit of what we now have to call *industrial* music (a cross of entertainment with performance art that guarantees the sort of spectacle huge audiences demand, in large part to lose themselves therein for a short while; though even here we have to be sure we're not confusing it with "industrial rock," a particular noise-based stylistic subset itself!). With this in mind, *non-commercial* music is quite viable. In terms of reception, I've somewhat jokingly used the term "unpopular music," but after the initial snicker it usually dies under the weight of its self-deprecation. A little more clear and realistic is *non-popular*, as it distinguishes this music from the larger field that dwarfs it (and most people know), and accepts the fact that it will always be the taste of a minority, even if an influential one. But it still has the feel of painting oneself into a corner.

Remaining sociological for a moment, it's worth realizing a very important thing about music written by people who call themselves "composers." *It tends to be made by individuals.* So much of the music industry nowadays is the result of large teams: performers, artists, songwriters, producers, managers, engineers, publicists, and market researchers. The artist in front is what the public sees and identifies with, but s/he, no matter how influential over the concept of his/her "brand," is still a bit of a figurehead.[7]

On the other hand, the piece that is *composed* tends to be created, using whatever means, by a human or perhaps a couple (as in composer/lyricist). As such, this is *artisanal* music. And as a consequence, it's naturally "retro," though we've already seen a whole series of trends in recent years where retro can become cool precisely because it defies certain norms of contemporary efficiency and sleekness (I'm old enough to enjoy the renewed interest in vinyl among those younger). It also unashamedly accepts the serious singer-songwriters into the fold. From the *troubadours* and *minnesingers* on, they've been always part of the mix. Adam de la Halle and Paul Simon would probably have a perfectly lovely conversation over lunch together. And who wouldn't want to be in the same room as Dylan?

Let's face it, composers are kind of nerdy. They move into the arcana of their field with a passionate engagement that's probably somewhere on the autistic spectrum. Fortunately for them, geek- and nerd-iness are cooler than ever, thanks to the success and style influence of those in the high-tech/code class. So "cutting-edge-oldfashionedness" may be something to embrace.

But after all is said and done, I've only limned the quarry, a little like the blind men describing the elephant. When I winnow through my own leavings, I find *postclassical, non-commercial, artisanal* retaining a particular resonance. We can keep them all in mind as we proceed. But we still don't have a single global term.

I feel there are two other, more comprehensive terms still in play, one that's been lurking behind the curtains and that you'll all recognize, the other a little more unexpected. The first is *art music*. It has a certain pretentiousness about its sound, but if we just accept that real art (partaking of the values I've enumerated above) can emerge from *any* language, tradition, or background, then I think it passes the test. For me it remains in the running, and I'll probably use it from time to time in what follows. But we have to be careful. The term can raise hackles, after several generations of its use to justify pretense, elitism, and exclusion.

And so I'm going to return to what we discovered earlier. *Survivable* music is written with the hope of a life that goes beyond its moment of birth, maybe even beyond the creator's life. It tends to have certain strengths of conception and construction that demonstrate exceptional craft and imagination, though these can be wildly diverse and mutually exclusive from one work to another. Its imagination delights and surprises us. It shows us things that we never conceived of, yet also seems like it's always been there, in the background. It's got ambition, and often moves into realms of abstraction that make its reception riskier. And it takes real work to make.

Survivable music is of course a goal, a hope. It wants to become *surviving* music. The odds are long that any composer will achieve it. It's a potential, not a guaranteed result. It probably would be better that we choose another term. But I don't know of another that better connects the ideal with the process for its achievement. Some will argue I'm just trying to slip *canon* back into the discourse by sleight of hand. Well, maybe so. But if such a collection of works moves into the future in a form that is more diverse than ever before, if it challenges the idea that it's the "property" of any single group, if it allows for constant revision and renewal—then why not? Let it be the touchstone, driving the inquiry and judgments of the remainder of my polemic. It's not perfect, but then nothing is. Maybe it's good enough for this journey.

2

The Gift That Keeps on Giving

From about 2005 to 2008 I became deeply involved—of my own volition—in a project that was literary and historical. I'd come to believe that Terry Riley's *In C* was a "stealth masterpiece," a work that was not only revolutionary as the "*Sacre*" of American musical minimalism but also incredibly ingenious in structure and economical of means. It was one of those things that wouldn't go away, even though on the surface it just *seemed* too simple to have had such an impact. And so (not stopping my own creative work, by the way) I went on a hunt for those who were part of the Bay Area arts scene of the early 1960s, who had participated in the work's 1964 San Francisco premiere, and in the 1968 recorded premiere in New York. Along with Riley, I met, interviewed, and got to know a little an extraordinary group of individuals including (but not only) Pauline Oliveros, David Behrman, Steve Reich, Morton Subotnick, Stuart Dempster, and Anna Halperin. Their freshness of perspective, openness of spirit, and lack of bitterness were an inspiration to me I still carry. The result was a book that came out in 2009.[1]

In September 2009, I was invited to be a keynote speaker at the Second International Conference on Minimalist Music, held in Kansas City. The central body of this chapter is adapted from that address. Its inclusion has a very focused reason: minimalism was perhaps the last great musical revolution we have seen in the art music tradition—the last time a seemingly dominant paradigm (in this case, the modernist/serialist that migrated to the United States from Europe over the mid-twentieth century) was overthrown in a tumultuous contest. I remember the controversy of the early works of Riley, Young, Reich, and Glass. It may have been the last period, at least for a while, that arguments could arise about whether a work was even "music" or not. Cage's chance revolution may have been even more threatening and controversial (in fact it still is), but it was also a bit earlier. Minimalism created the Great Divide of postwar American music, Uptown versus Downtown. It also performed a contradictory double action, on the one hand defying and undermining the ruling order and, on the other hand, simultaneously initiating a process that would lead to a rapprochement of contemporary practices with those more traditional (again, the very definition of the avant-garde suggested in the previous chapter). This double function makes it particularly important to consider as we consider the convergences I will examine ahead. And for those who will stick with me through the course of this entire text, you'll find several fields of inquiry raised that will be examined in chapters to come. With that in mind, here's the essence of my address, followed by thoughts that it now occasions in retrospect.

* * *

In early 1963, Terry Riley was living in Paris, making a living as a jazz and ragtime pianist traveling from one US army base to another . . . or taking off for a few weeks to southern Spain and northern Africa to listen to Arab music and smoke *kief* . . . or joining a traveling circus and accompanying acrobats and sword-swallowers. Along with these adventures, he was approached by an old Bay Area friend, the director and impresario Ken Dewey, to make the music for a multimedia theater project titled *The Gift*. Riley immediately warmed to the task, especially when he found out that the jazz trumpeter Chet Baker, an idol of his and just released from jail in Lucca, Italy, after serving a sentence for drug possession, would be involved. Riley quickly conceived to use Baker and his combo's playing for an experimental soundtrack. And he, having already made a number of pioneering tape pieces involving echo and overdubbing (above all, *Mescalin Mix* [1960–62]), made a stunning discovery as he began to sketch the piece. Thanks to access to the French national radio studios, he collaborated with some of the engineers there. In the process, he found that by threading tape through two successive tape recorders, one could record a sound on the first, the second would play it back at a time interval determined by the distance between the two, and the first would then record *that* playback. And so on, in a recursive loop that would continue until the connection from #1 to #2 was cut. The piece was called *Music for The Gift*.[2] This sort of delay-texture is by now so familiar to us that we barely notice it. Yet remember this was 1963. There was almost nothing like it at the time, and certainly nothing as visible. Riley himself has said this piece was critical in two ways: it was his first "orchestral" work, even though it was written for the tape medium, and it was the last step necessary to unlock the secret of repetition and the manipulation of modules he perfected in *In C*.

So if *In C* is one of the founding documents of American musical minimalism, it came about because Riley was given a "gift"—one that came from an intersection of his eclectic musical interests and upbringing, the development of technology, and being in the right place at the right moment. And in turn minimalism has given a series of gifts back to music—gifts that have nourished, revived, and transformed the development of new music, and whose nature are perhaps only starting to become apparent as we now are plunged deep into *this* century. Minimalism has been credited with re-introducing into musical practice pulse, repetition, consonance, triadic harmony, modality, trance and ritual . . . and on and on. And all of those points are valid, but to stop there suggests that a set of technical and stylistic markers, most of them present in older music, were reaffirmed, and now music could get back to its more traditional roots. It makes minimalism a kind of aesthetic stalking horse that preceded a more valid and conservative "return to sense." Yes, devices like extremely slow harmonic motion could be acknowledged as radical, but they also could be seen as reactive excesses that would pass after the first phase of the movement. This approach makes minimalism essentially a reactive project, one that slew big bad modernism and gave us a new, more user-friendly form of romanticism. There *is* truth to this, and one need look no further than the music of John Adams to see the result . . . and I'm not being snide or critical, because I admire his music greatly, and think it's a grand body of work. He's fulfilled this "reclamation" agenda for minimalism brilliantly. But if minimalism has any larger, more progressive legacy, any gift more significant than merely "giving us back" traditional musical practice after a century's bout of temporary insanity, then we need to shift our perspective and look from other angles to find what is truly innovative therein, and what it can give us to help generate a genuinely new musical practice for this century. And not too surprisingly, I see *In C* as one of the most important harbingers and models for that practice.

But before I explore these regions, I need to make a brief and personal detour. Indeed, a sort of confession. When I first encountered minimalism, it was in the early 1970s, when I was an undergraduate. I wasn't a music major, but I was aching to enter in that world, and was making a fairly tempestuous transition to get there. I was in love with the music of Ives, Ruggles, and other American Ultramodernists, and at the time the increasing complexity of composers such as Elliott Carter seemed the natural outgrowth of that tradition. So minimalism was perplexing and indeed threatening. It seemed too *easy*, anti-intellectual (or maybe not intellectual enough), and yes rather druggy. It scared me a little. I picked up a copy of the LP of *In C* around 1974, and dutifully listened. And indeed, it became more intriguing to me when, while playing it on vacation at home, my father came into room to demand, "Turn down that crap!" As I said, it suddenly became more interesting. But still it felt alien and alienating.

Of course I've changed over time, as we all do. My relation to minimalism is now a happy one, where the beauties of this repertoire are evident. Part of this is simply the balm of historical distance, which mutes the power of controversies to wound us. Part of it is just a greater maturity of a human who's accepted more of his strengths and weaknesses. But perhaps the biggest part is what those younger than me see in it. *They* see minimalism as a natural element in the musical landscape, a historical style and technical toolbox, and have no idea what the big fuss was about. And as we'll see in a bit, they also have a handle on surprising facets of the legacy.

So I've taken a moment to lay this out as a case study. Its subject—me—is a composer who isn't by any stretch classed as a minimalist. But over time I've come to understand in a visceral way what minimalism has bequeathed to all of us, and I've learned from it as an artist. Perhaps a composer like myself, distant in some ways from the movement, but critically open, and of another generation (transitional—after the "classic" phase but still close enough to understand many issues viscerally, unlike the current youngest creative generation) may be able to offer fresh insights.

Detour complete, we're back on the main route. So then, what *are* these broader "gifts" of minimalism? There are a host of such, and to try to narrow this *will* inevitably be an oversimplification. Nevertheless, I'll stick my neck out. I see four gifts: *flow, layering, sensuality,* and *openness*.

The first two are by far the most obvious and connect most to the standard catalogue of attributes for the movement. *Flow* suggests the way that music moves through time. Is it continuous or discontinuous? There is no doubt that by the mid-twentieth century, the most visible forms of contemporary concert music in the classical tradition had a rhythmic template that emphasized disruption, contrast, even spasm. At the beginning of the century, it had a deep and true rationale—the exploration of the sub- and un-conscious realms unearthed by the new psychology, a climate that fostered the extraordinary aesthetic discoveries of Expressionism. (And there was also the embrace of what was then called the "primitive" cultures outside of the West, or of folk culture outside of Western high art, which opened up alternative, irregular pulsating fields.) But by the time art music in America had reached the 1950s and 1960s, much of the original context had been lost for these expressive tropes. We weren't in Europe, it wasn't the end of a Silver Age, and despite all the best attempts of American intellectuals and artists, people just weren't as neurotic as in Vienna on the eve of the First World War. The most visible music from about 1950 on came to be about "gesture," but that meant that everything of interest tended to be on the surface. (Or at least everything audible; the structures of serialism tried to create a broader and deeper architecture analogous to tonality, but the fate of that project is by now all too apparent.)

Minimalism's response was obvious—pulse returned, pattern returned, repetition returned. Repeated patterns became motives, leading either to more traditional-sounding results or a new and more radical sort of "wallpaper" that suggested the abstract decorative arts of non-Western cultures. But no matter what the approach, in minimalist music we learned to *breathe* again. Music, which had become cramped, demanding a level of moment-to-moment concentration that was exhausting even for the committed acolyte, reaffirmed timescales more attuned to natural human rhythms of attention and information processing. Of course, "classic" minimalism, the initial response to the modernist/expressionist template, was itself a counterreaction that at times created temporal expanses so vast as to suggest an entirely different, previously unknown way of listening and processing, one that put off many otherwise open listeners at the start. Indeed, there were many pieces from this period and approach that in fact expanded to such lengths that an entirely new concept of *scale* entered into the temporal dimension of Western music (think Young, Glass, and even later Feldman). When pieces moved into durations of hours, a curious paradox emerged. On the one hand, to listen, one had to give up expectation, and one had to go into the moment. By dropping teleology, any sound that one encountered became a world unto itself, fresh and new. Yet at the same time, placed in this immense context, these sounds *also* evoked a trope of infinitude, and one looked out over the entire landscape. One lived in the time of the moment, but also in the time of eternity. The local and the global now coexisted, but in a remarkable state where the middle ground had disappeared. As in some meditative practices, a creative paradox was concretely embodied.

This capacity to enfold simultaneously two such different realities suggests the second gift, *layering*. This may seem a little contradictory, because in the visual arts, in particular painting, the term "minimalism" suggested flatness, the refusal of a painting to be anything other than a two-dimensional field on which color and light played out their lives (something that was ironically also emerging concurrently in the later works of such Abstract Expressionists as Mark Rothko and Ad Reinhardt). But in music, as we've just seen, minimalism—unlike serialism—created a field of action in which different things could be heard simultaneously, *really* heard. Those very things could be very different, coming from different aesthetic-technical stances: LaMonte Young's *Trio for Strings* (1958) could be heard as a series of drones, but also as a glacially unfolding tone-row; Steve Reich's phasing could be an intricate hocketing clockwork counterpoint in the moment, *and* the cycling of materials against one another over longer timespans (a "gradual process" as he called it, like the movement of watch's minute hand, invisible in the moment yet evident over a longer period); and Phil Glass's blur of notes could be an unvarying soundmass, but also the surface of huge tonal movements with Brucknerian pacing. And of course Riley's *In C* could be simultaneously heard as a jangling carnival texture; a tidal progression through various modes and harmonic centers, against a steady C drone; and a "flexible canon" of tightly defined and developed motives. The interplay between concept and artifact, and process and product—so important to the emergence of conceptual art—is obviously at play here, but there's also layering—or we might better say *multiplicity*. (Note the non-hierarchical tone of that term.) And—a very important point—that multiplicity is *concrete* and *audible*, embodied in the notes themselves. Extramusical rationales (timelessness, trance, non-Western, etc.), even if evoked, were never necessary for the music to have a real, palpable effect. There's a fundamental honesty at work: *what you get is what you hear.*

And with such sonic realism and honesty comes the third gift, *sensuality*. Let's not dismiss modernism totally here; there was in its best works a great bracing energy, athleticism, and searing intensity. And there are masterpieces of this twentieth-century aesthetic that *will* survive. But for the vast majority of pieces written under its influence, I think it's fair to say that the listening experience could not be described as "pleasant." Indeed most modernist composers were repelled by that term, which they saw as dishonest to the zeitgeist. Thus, your "typical" modernist work was at the least phenomenologically *abrasive*.

Now it's true that some of the earliest works of minimalism were austere and streamlined in the extreme. But they were never ugly. If they were reductive, it was in the pursuit of purity. But beauty, so long suspect in the modernist viewpoint, made a comeback with minimalism. Not for nothing was one of its leading record labels named Lovely Music. Pulsating masses of sound where overtones, difference tones, and phantom tones began to emerge from seemingly simple textures was a type of magic, a conjuring of sonic spirits from the ether. This could be laid-back and hypnotic, or it could be rambunctiously athletic. For me, *In C* seems to encapsulate both of these qualities. On the one hand, there's a "gamelanian" timelessness about it (even though at the time he wrote it, Riley had not yet heard a note of Indonesian music). On the other, there's a sense of unbridled joy, a childlike, leaping ecstasy that can be harnessed any which way by the players and their choices. I can tell you after years of living with the piece, there are moments that bring tears to my eyes, their arrival having been so anticipated, the pacing in certain performances so right and inevitable. (And then in others, with completely different performer decisions, they can be a pleasurable shock, despite our knowing that their appearance is imminent.) This pleasure principle only seems to be increasing. As you listen to successive recordings and performances of *In C*, culminating in the huge forty-fifth anniversary birthday bash in April 2009 at Carnegie Hall, there seems to be a mounting understanding of how much sheer *fun* is embodied in the piece—pleasure, beauty, joy. Obviously the twentieth century had to be *really* bad in order to force us to give these up for so long.

And that brings us to the fourth gift, *openness*. This would seem but an extension of previous items, if we interpreted the term as vastness, on the sort of geographic scale often referenced when we talk of American music. But I'm talking about a different sort of "open," and it's this aspect to which my students have clued me in.

I'm speaking of openness as the capacity to simultaneously accept music coming from radically different practices, in particular those which attempt to fix the musical event in advance with as much precision as possible, *and* those which trust to conditions embodied in the moment of performance (intuition, chance, environment). In its simplest form, it can be boiled down to notated vs. improvised music. And, I've discovered that for my students, one of the most prominent markers of a new, twentieth-century (and twenty-first century) practice is an acceptance of improvisation as a natural part of the "traditional" composer's toolkit. It's interesting to me that while both jazz and indeterminate/aleatoric (i.e., Cageian) music are interesting and useful to them, what seems to engage them the most is something different yet again. It tends to be openness that is algorithmically structured. "Generative music" is a term I'm hearing from them a lot, and it works from the premise of a few basic rules being chosen and put into relation with one another, without a certain idea of the result. The rules tend to be strict, often simple, but the results can be quite extravagant and unanticipated.

(In the visual realm, one of my favorite manifestations is the computer-generated drawings of Stephen Wolfram's *A New Kind of Science*.[3]) The result doesn't have to be more complex either—a good deal of Enoesque ambient music can result, as well as very strange and groovy techno riffs. There are a number of programs out there that tap into this practice (Max is the one I'm most familiar with, but hardly the only one), and in fact this *does* seem to be evidence of that other great contemporary sea-change: the technological revolution that now rocks our world every week. The musical product of this approach seems to have connections to chaos theory, to the way genetic evolution selects through constant accidental mutation that paradoxically leads to seemingly "planned" results, and to theories of developing consciousness in artificial intelligence.

Strange as it might seem, this is where I see *In C* exerting its greatest potential future influence. In my book I speak of it ultimately as a piece of *software*. By that I mean that the piece—embodied in its precisely calibrated score of one page, fifty-three modules—is a network of data (the motives) and rules (the "intuitive-canonic" structure) set into action. In the course of the piece, every single note and rhythm will be predetermined by the information in the score. But of course the flow, shape, texture, duration, poetry, and drama of the work will only emerge as the players follow the rules, by listening to one another, in real time, collectively, carefully, creatively. It's a model of how strict structure and serendipity can coexist.

Not that Terry Riley was thinking all this when he heard the piece in his head that fateful spring night in 1964, as he was taking the bus home to Potrero Hill from the Gold Street Saloon, after a long night of ragtime piano playing. But like many, many things embodied in his art and life, he was onto something ahead of the game. He's of course not the only such one. To take just one example, the phasing one hears in Reich's early works, when the two instruments start to move apart, sounds genuinely chaotic for a brief span before the new precise rhythmic texture kicks in, yet it comes out of a completely strict, deterministic process. Interestingly enough, two composers closely associated with the premiere recording of *In C*, David Behrman (the producer) and David Rosenboom (who played viola) have been some of the most important explorers of this realm between the raw and the cooked, using the computer from very early on as a partner in the creative process. But *In C*, even though it uses no high technology, is one of the first truly successful examples of a fruitful creative paradox. On the one hand, it shows how an artist can exert precise control in a realm outside of real time—a realm of abstract structure and identifiable personal stamp that is clearly recognizable with each new iteration. Yet on the other, it *relinquishes* that control to allow all who take it up ("composer" included) to explore her/his intimate, personal musical space; a region of play, accident, and instinct; a world embodied in the *now*.

If anything is fundamental to the American musical tradition, it's this "opening up" to the moment. We hear it in so many of our greatest composers from the origins of our concert tradition—Ives, Ellington, Cage, Mingus, Gershwin, (Theolonius . . . and also Meredith!) Monk. Minimalism, despite its initial critique as being soulless and mechanistic, in fact is another step in this progress of embracing a world that cannot be totally dominated, accepting our place in it, engaging in a dance with it. As such, I suspect it's the first time since the Florentine Camerata that we've had a truly seismic shift in musical aesthetics, and one of whose implications we yet have no clear idea. (Listening to Monteverdi around 1610, would you really have been able to imagine the sound of Mahler?) Perhaps it even holds the key to how the extraordinary abstract and architectural advances of modernism will find new and fresh life as well. Whatever the case it's the first time the shift has come from this side of the Atlantic—indeed, I should correct myself, because the true origins of the shift are on the Pacific Coast. This is something that those of us as Americans can take a little pride in . . . but we'd better not get too self-congratulatory: it's a gift given without strings to the world, out of our hands. It's reflecting and reverberating throughout and between cultures, coming back to us in surprising new forms, going globally viral as we speak.

* * *

Four years after having written this address, my feelings about the place of minimalism in the evolution of late-twentieth and early-twenty-first-century concert music remain largely the same. The point about "openness," in fact, now appears even more significant to me than ever, to the point of requiring a separate chapter in this book. But I think if we are to posit any sort of "emerging common practice," it's critical now to explore a few more thoughts about rhythm and musical time that were broached earlier in the section on *flow*. These demand the following general (and highly personal) survey.

One of greatest legacies of the twentieth century has been the return of pulse to art music. The nineteenth century is full of grand rhythmic structures and innovations, and from Schubert to Schumann to Mendelssohn to Brahms, there is an idealized quality of *dance* that breathes life into so much of their music. But ultimately, all temporal relations in music come down to two factors, each derived from human bodily process. On the one hand, there is the *pulse*, which comes from the heartbeat, and, on the other, there is the *phrase*, which comes from the act of breathing. In the nineteenth century, the latter achieved a prominence, architecture and sophistication that had not been seen since the High Renaissance. It's not for nothing that despite having existed for two centuries prior, opera really takes off in the romantic era, when the majority of its core repertoire is written. Likewise, symphonic music grows in scale until by the end of century an hour-long symphony is no longer unthinkable, but instead increasingly the norm (of course the development of similarly vast and sophisticated harmonic architectures partner with expanded phrase-rhythm to make this possible).

At the beginning of the twentieth century, it appeared that this breath-based stranglehold was broken, by the emergence of a series of landmark works with a renewed predominance of pulse, though now in asymmetric rearrangements. Stravinsky's *Le Sacre de Printemps* is the avatar, but in countless other composers who are writing some of the most popular and groundbreaking works in the era of roughly 1905–30—Bartók, *Les Six*, Prokofiev, Copland, Gershwin, Hindemith, Weill—rhythms that emerge from the encounter with folk and popular music gave back an "edge" that concert music had almost lost. It could be a cubistic fracturing of regular patterns that was perceived as a quality of folk and non-Western music, or it could be that of the syncopated swing of jazz.

But simultaneously there was a counter-conception of rhythm emerging in Central European Expressionism that privileged gesture over pulse. We hear it in the early operas and tone poems of Strauss, but it comes to fullest fruition in Schoenberg and the Second Viennese School, especially the "middle" or "free atonal" period. As a metaphor of the anguish, confusion, and fundamental moral ambivalence of the era prior to and emerging from the First World War, it is unrivaled, in fact a sound of genius to match its time. This was music whose flow was based on the idea of its opposite, *disruption*. This paradox had its own exhilaration, and it couldn't help but feel revolutionary.

And then, after the ultimate cataclysm of the Second World War, something strange happened. The system Schoenberg had developed to control pitch and harmony (having himself been concerned by the seeming anarchy he had loosed with intuitive atonality), *dodecaphonic serialism*, became united with the early expressionist rhythmic language as a new sort of International Style.

The original passion of that rhythmic stance was cooled by its encounter with the more rational, ordered ethos of serialism, and in fact the gestural template became a surface beneath which even temporal elements could be ordered in the same manner as pitches. It was a strange marriage, and its purest form—integral serialism—only lasted a decade or two in Europe.

But with the migration of many European masters during the war to the United States and their entrance into the academy, it was given new life and influence. Of course, music free from both serial planning and gestural stasis was still being written throughout the period, but there's no doubt that it did not have the cachet of the imported model, especially when two composers most associated with rhythmic innovation and extra-classical roots, "converted"— Stravinsky and Copland. By the early 1960s the only great outliers were Cage and his school, though ironically much of the music created by chance procedures (e.g., the monumental *Music of Changes*; 1951) actually had a strangely similar surface sound to many of the hyper-calculated monuments of the era (think Boulez's *Structures* Book I; 1952). It in fact performed an act of brilliant subversion, but in more of a conceptual manner (similar sound from a polar-opposite practice) than a concretely aural one.

This is where things stood just after 1960, when minimalism produced its first masterpieces. The movement did not invent its rhythmic practice out of whole cloth, but it was exceptional in being attuned to the intersection of a series of changes that were banging on the concert hall door. One was the need for a return to the great rhythmic drive of the early twentieth century. Another was a growing awareness of the richness of music traditions outside of Western practice. And finally, there was the overwhelming rise of a new energy embodied first in jazz, and then even more primally in rock. Each one of the "Fab Four" of this movement had interests and experience outside of the classically trained norm: LaMonte Young was a brilliant jazz saxophonist; Terry Riley a virtuosic jazz pianist, an early devotee of Indian and North African music, and—perhaps the least known point—a lover of the music of Poulenc; Steve Reich a jazz drummer who voyaged to West Africa to study drumming; Phil Glass, the most traditional conservatory product, who went to India and flipped out over his close encounter with Ravi Shankar. In short, all four composers personified in their interests, explorations, and tastes, the set of changing parameters by which young musicians were really experiencing and judging music.

And once we have reached the advent of minimalism by the 1970s, we are basically to the place we are today. The music unleashed by the movement, both its own enduring successes and those influenced by it, has entered into the repertoire. It has not obliterated everything else, but it *has* cast most of the other musical languages of the twentieth century in a new light, and caused us to retrospectively re-evaluate them. What it has done to our understanding of contemporary rhythm is profound, and I see this occurring in two areas.

First, the return of pulse, pattern, and repetition reinvigorated classical practice and allowed a new "grooviness" back into the concert hall. Of all the second-generation minimalists (whom now are acknowledged as "postminimalists"), John Adams has been the most expansive in his adoption and reinterpretation of these gifts. Probably no composer living has done more to revivify the type of energy in orchestral music that we heard in early Stravinsky. It's of course different, happily. The great surging polyrhythmic textures he creates often have the effect more of a gigantic wave of sound than the throbbing dances of Stravinsky in the great early ballets. But if you look at the scores, you see Adams has learned his lessons from his ancestor and inflected the techniques toward minimalism's more open, hypnotic aesthetic. One of his lesser known scores remains for me a nearly ideal example of this synthesis, the two-movement *El Dorado*[4] (1991), an orchestral "hell and heaven" portrait of California that starts with dark stabbing violence and ends with Edenic ecstasy. Adams has never stopped growing and questing in technique, and not just on the rhythmic level; his harmonic language has become evermore chromatic, and he bridles nowadays if he's called a minimalist. There's justification in this, but his roots are clearly in that practice, and he's shown how it can be reintegrated with aspects of earlier ones worth saving.

A slightly more populist manifestation of this is the world of post-minimal music that draws energy from rock. Post-Zappa, the music of the composers who founded the Bang on a Can empire (Michael Gordon, Julia Wolfe, and David Lang) has not only advanced the idea of a hybrid rock-classical music, far more sophisticated than previous experiments in the field that came mostly from the rock end in the 1970s and 1980s, but also created a kind of "brand" that is advanced through their policy of presentation and commissioning.[5] Of the three, I've been most taken by the work of Gordon. It can be very hit-or-miss, but it's ambitious, and when it does hit the mark, it's with a wallop. His soundtrack to Bill Morrissey's *Decasia* (2001) is a crazed perpetual crescendo that comes closer to Xenakis than almost any other American music I know. *Yo Shakespeare*[6] (1992) is notable for rhythms that are propulsive and yet highly complex, irregular, and asymmetric. Gordon seems to me a great example of music whose rhythmic profile is *irregular yet periodic*. I mean by that a vocabulary of durations and patterns that can be quite complex, yet which cycles in a way so that one hears a groove nonetheless. This is not totally new: earlier in the twentieth century, Olivier Messiaen had already figured out this trick, and in fact his music looks more influential than ever as a result.

The upshot is that despite its initial manifestation as music of unparalleled (surface) simplicity, minimalism, *by that very reduction and economy of components*, opened up a field for renewed experiment. Steve Reich embodies this point in the course of his evolution. From the simplest sounds and ideas (two hands clapping, with rotation of a rhythmic module against its fixed form), he added new techniques to his toolkit piece by piece, until the masterpiece *Music For 18 Musicians* (1976) could emerge, with its additive melodies, phasing, and canons. Finally, this approach is not restricted to the concert hall. Much music of techno and Electronic Dance Music strikes me as a natural extension of this investigation of "complex grooviness."

That is the first legacy of minimalism's impact on musical time. It both returns music to primal sources that have nourished the art music tradition from its very beginning and opens up that practice to other languages and traditions that had become increasingly excluded during the nineteenth and twentieth centuries. The second legacy is something more radical, and we are only starting to cope with its implications.

As mentioned above, minimalism changed music's temporal *scale* dramatically, and probably forever. Though its duration is never fixed, *In C* usually clocks in comfortably on either side of an hour. Philip Glass already had explored extended musical landscapes in such works as *Music in Twelve Parts* (1971–74), but he hit a nerve when he conceived *Einstein on the Beach* (1976) as a four-hour shifting three-dimensional slideshow of surreal tableaux (though as much because of his interaction with the glacial theatrical pacing of Robert Wilson). And though he is not usually typed as a minimalist, Morton Feldman represents a unique take, a kind of modernist variant, similar in music to what his painter friend Mark Rothko was doing late in life, stripping down to essences while paradoxically expanding the field of play. When we reach Feldman's six-hour String Quartet No.2 (1983), as listeners we are entering into a landscape or environment, not just a piece. Things happen, things change over time, but time is so stretched that it's difficult to discern a narrative.[7]

The release of musical time into a new, vaster space suggested an approach closer to that of extended rituals in non-Western cultures, where the needs of community or supernatural forces would be satisfied only when consensus or a sign from above confirmed completion. In short, the use of music as a tool of *meditation*, lost in the West pretty much since the Middle Ages, began its return. There are many works now that trade in this expanded-time ethos: I just heard one recently, Gordon's *Timber* for six percussionists on tuned wooden bars, lasting about an hour.[8] But the impact actually resonates even more beyond the concert hall, in two ways.

The first is the emergence of *ambient music*. This is music that does not attempt to create an enclosed aesthetic event, but instead presents an environment into which one enters simply to listen, and through listening, to give up expectations of teleology (goal-direction). It has led to a lot of New Age pabulum, but it also has stimulated many composers to realize their most radical visions. This *can* still occur in the concert hall, but the manner of listening is of necessity radically different. Many of Cage's works, especially later ones such as *Ryoanji* (1983–85), *Roaratorio* (1979), and the "number" pieces,[9] create this sense of entering the timeless. And though they are a natural extension of his lifelong practice, it's intriguing that these pieces come later in his life, after minimalism had displaced modernism as the dominant avant-garde aesthetic.[10] Likewise, the lifelong pursuit of "deep listening" by Pauline Oliveros takes this a step further into a fully formed aesthetic and practice. Her *Sonic Meditations* (1974) are a starting point for communal activity by performers both professional and amateur, with no one privileged. All are allowed to explore and discover aural phenomena and create without holding any "rights" to the final product. In this way a new sort of musical "democracy" emerges that demands commitment and musicianship but doesn't make a fetish of traditionally conceived virtuosity. And as an exemplar of a second- or third-generation minimalist aesthetic, John Luther Adams has created pieces that by their very nature attempt to evoke Nature itself, rather than merely depict it. Part of that comes from strict processes, whose result is more important as the proof of their existence than as an artifact in its own right (*Strange and Sacred Noise*, 1991–97); open structures that give flexibility of relations between component parts (*Inuksuit*, 2009); and scale that suggests ancestors such as Feldman (*For Lou Harrison*, 2004; *Veils*, 2005).[11]

The second emerging aspect of music on a new level of scale is *installation*. In this case the idea of the piece having *any* aspect of closure is put aside. Instead, the listener enters into a sonic environment that is ongoing. It may be triggered by her presence, it may be responding to other outside stimuli, or it may consist of elements that interact and modify one another indefinitely, as a mobile form (but a potentially mutating one). This may seem ironic, even mistaken, considering the fact that over and over we hear that contemporary life temporally fragments our sense of existence. We are multitasking, rushed beyond endurance, our attention-spans frayed to breaking. How can exactly the opposite have any use or relevance in such a culture? The answer here is simple: as refuge. The more we descend into a vortex of conflicting demands and fractured time, the more we yearn for the space to experience time unmediated, to feel it as a sort of infinite space. As the church was a refuge from the violence and brutality of life in the Middle Ages, so the expanded time of installation may be an escape from the frazzling present.

Here again, J. L. Adams has made a definitive contribution with *The Place Where You Go to Listen* in the Museum of the North at University of Alaska Fairbanks. This piece (described in an important *New Yorker* profile by Alex Ross[12]) is a room where meteorological and seismological data from all over Alaska is collected, and then translated into sonic and visual effects via a sophisticated Max patch. In Adams's case, his role is not so much that of traditional composer, as rather a translator/editor/designer of an interface between natural phenomena and sonic markers thereof. There's no question that this is a "composition," but it's also unlike any ever experienced before. And there are an increasing number of such approaches, from a wide range of composers on the aesthetic spectrum. This is one of the most important shifts in contemporary musical practice, and so I'll return to installation when I explore sound art under the rubrics of *openness* and *sonic essentialism* further on in these chapters.

To sum up, there are many "gifts" of minimalism, which even now feels like the single most recent avant-garde revolution art music has experienced (and it's an inverse proof of its revolutionary impact that so much of it now is mainstream). Its gifts to our sense of rhythm and the unfolding of musical time have shifted our perceptions on the subject more than I think we realize.[13] And this is a deeply *American* gift. It's waiting for a complement in the realm of pitch and harmony and that will be coming soon from across the Atlantic, as explained a couple of chapters ahead.

3

Left to Our Own Devices

Ever notice how now *everyone* you see (especially on a college campus) is tied to a phone and either wired up or bent toward it in an attitude to submissive prayer? I'm joking, but not much. Every generation likes to think that it has seen the most dramatic changes in culture and lifestyle of any before. The current one is no exception, even though the generation of my grandparents (born at the start of the twentieth century) may have seen even greater change—they witnessed the appearance of the electric light, the telephone, sound recording (in all its iterations and generations), the airplane and jet travel, satellite communications, and extraterrestrial travel. But what we *do* have now is an extrapolation from many of those breakthroughs, so that it surpasses even our imaginations at an exponential rate. And where there is a *real* revolution is in communications and information; *it* is changing not just our physical reality, but even more so the nature of how we think and experience our lives. And its impact on music, for a long time trumpeted but seeming a little overblown, has finally reached such a critical mass that its impact is indisputable, no matter how pro or con one stands toward it.

By this point it's clear that any musician simply *has* to come to grips with technology, in part because it has worked out such intuitive user-interfaces. One has no longer any excuse to ignore or not use it. No matter how "conservative," a composer will find beneficial ways to incorporate technology into his practice (and remember that the nineteenth-century explosion of instrumental innovation that brought about the present-day orchestra was itself an "analog" technological revolution). So I'd like to examine the ways it has changed our musical life, as these changes in turn become essential aids toward meeting the series of challenges I'll enumerate ahead.

Music technology has changed the very act of writing music. It's very rare that I find any younger musician nowadays who doesn't use a notation program such as Finale or Sibelius. If one takes the time and effort to master the subtleties, it gives a final product that can be the equal of any traditionally engraved edition, to the point that even all commercially published music is now produced digitally (and indeed traditional publication is under siege, since anyone has the potential to produce a professional-standard score). Even if one uses non-standard, extended, or graphic notation, programs have reached a level of sophistication that even these can emerge in better form than by hand alone. In these special cases, a combination of the handmade and the digital is more possible than ever, thanks to scanning and editing via programs designed for the visual arts, such as Photoshop.

Performers now expect this visual product; it's a standard that is a mark of professionalism that reassures them. It also looks like the repertoire they are already used to playing. And, quite simply, it's easier to read than any but the most immaculate hand (the extraordinary layout and calligraphy of George Crumb being the gold standard that very few can ever match). It really was not that long ago (in fact, in my early career) that most composers worked with ink on lined vellum, correcting mistakes with razor blades and typewriter erasers, reproducing these autograph scores at blueprint services. It now sounds roughly equivalent to the horse-and-carriage, and in retrospect it was.

An even more dramatic reduction of labor occurs in the production of parts. Notation programs save the score not only as an integral document, but as a series of potential subdocuments embodied in each instrumental/vocal line. These can be instantaneously extracted. In most cases there still needs to be careful attention to formatting and presentation, and glitches can still cause errors and omissions to slip through. As a result, a "parts copyist" who is really an extractor/editor, is useful, but s/he is now more of a luxury than necessity. A composer, especially a poor one, can now do the whole job if she has to, at a fraction of the time and money such a commitment would have mandated before.

The mention of correction brings up editing. This is perhaps an even greater innovation than the return of the engraved standard. Now any change can be incorporated into a score and saved with a single keystroke; not just local changes—a pitch here, a dynamic there—but global ones. Entire sections can be deleted, added, and moved via cut-and-paste. As a result, revising scores is far simpler, and there is no longer the barrier of excruciating and endless labor demanded earlier. Composers thought twice about such revisions before; now no longer. That excuse has vanished.

Yet another consequence that emerges is that a piece no longer has to exist in only one version. This is a more radical shift of composer consciousness.

It gives increasing freedom to make alternate versions of a work for different circumstances. Pieces may be reorchestrated or rearranged with an ease and freedom never before known. This increasingly "modular" idea of the work is one of the ways by which the aforementioned greater "openness" emerges.

And a final implication of the new software is the immediate aural feedback it provides. I will say that one of my most notable experiences of change in teaching is the format of the private lesson. For decades a student brought in music on paper, and then we flailed through it at the piano. Now they plug into a little sound system in the office and let it rip. My job has become much more like that of a critic as a result—good for me, since I'm a modest pianist but a good critic! For the composer in the act of writing, there is no longer any lag time between conception, notation, and audition. The key is Musical Instrument Digital Interface (MIDI), a standard that has now been with us since the 1980s and allows communication between one digital sound component and another.[1] Originally the flow would be from electronic keyboard to computer to some sort of "black box" sound-library, but by now such is always solely software-based. The sounds available range from irredeemably cheesy to scarily convincing (depending on the amount of cash one is willing to invest), and the computer still lacks the human "touch" that subtly randomizes a host of parameters in generating a performance. But it gets better all the time, and those who predict it will never reach a convincing human level are probably dreaming. At present, if a composer has a good aural imagination, he can listen past the sonic limitations in the studio, using the MIDI interface as the equivalent of the piano short score of previous generations. Issues of harmony, counterpoint, tempo, pacing, overall formal shape, and flow can all be assessed now in real time. Not only can this be useful for composers of any level of skill and experience, but for young composers it can accelerate the learning process enormously, a sort of aural-conceptual feedback loop that allows immediate evaluation of any idea, a sort of "living sketch."

And at this point, I must also hoist a warning flag. The advantages of this new approach are evident and multiple, as detailed above. But there are dangers as well. With this exceptional ease of production, it's easy for a beginning composer to write anything, hear it, and bask in the joy thereof. The initial thrill is a wonderful thing, but if one is not careful, it can short-circuit essential critical faculties and lead to believing a first draft is final.

Another danger is something quite idiomatic to the medium. As one composes, the music spreads out before one in a "scroll" format. Thus, the composer is limited to only what can be viewed of any portion of a work, determined by monitor size. If one shifts to page view, one still only sees one page at a time. As a result, the *global* conception of the piece, something possible with a sheaf of completed score pages laid out, is denied to the composer's perspective. And as a result, form, that is musical architecture, can suffer. I hear more and more pieces that have the quality of a stream of consciousness, one idea morphing into the next, but without a comprehensive armature that defines their successive meaning to one another. This is in part I think a consequence of the software. This is not a reason to avoid the new technology or adopt a Luddite stance, but it *is* reason for caution, and awareness of things potentially sacrificed for progress on other fronts. Thus the inculcation of critical thinking concerning the use of creative technology can be an important aspect of formal study, and a reason that such training still has value.[2]

But we've not even left the composer's studio yet. Technology is far more visible (and audible) as we move into performance. The overarching principle is that the different facets of sound in concert expand into new dimensions; in short, we now have a whole new school of orchestration based on the digital. The idea that there are multiple *palettes* and *platforms* for the expansion of the timbral universe parses out into the following:

1) Ever since Varèse wrote *Déserts* (1954), the possibility of combining live performance with pre-existent soundtracks has been an avenue into a new blend between sounds formally excluded from the concert hall and those already admitted. We'd had sounds earlier from live sources, such as the siren in *Ionisation* (1931) or the airplane propeller in Antheil's *Ballet Mécanique* (1924), but these are still treated as isolated instruments, not an equal partner in the sonic landscape (Varèse's 1923 *Hyperprism*, with its antiphonal ensembles of percussion and winds, comes closer to this equation). Luigi Russolo and the Italian Futurists posited a complete orchestra of "noise-maker" instruments (*intonarumori*) even earlier, but they petered out as influences, and have only come back into view with renewed historical interest.

   Varèse's model in *Déserts* uses more abstract pre-recorded sounds, and works such as Roberto Gerhard's Third Symphony (1960) and Babbitt's *Correspondences* (1967) are further examples of this approach, though the sound of electronic sounds divorced from any *concrete* context seems to have fallen out of favor nowadays. Rather, recorded sounds coming out of recognizable aural experience begin to merge with the acoustic palette only with the nightingale in Respighi's *The Pines of Rome* (1924). Cage's *Imaginary Landscape No.4* (1951) for a dozen radios is a remarkable blend of the most concrete sounds imaginable—random radio broadcasts—with the abstract principle of chance-driven selection. A brilliant, more contemporary extension of the idea is Steve Reich's *Different Trains* (1988), where vocal tracks edited to create particular speech-rhythm patterns provide a constant backdrop to motoric string quartet writing (an idea pursued further in his 1994 *City Life* and 2002 *Three Tales*).[3]

In sum, the entry of formerly "ordinary" sound (speech, nature, quotidian life) is now not only a part of the orchestrational palette but due to increasing precision for loading and triggering such soundfiles (once via sampler keyboard but now by laptop), they begin to act like any other instrument in an ensemble. Perhaps most significantly (and this applies to each of the technological interventions described below, as well), the advent of this sound-palette inevitably enlarges the timbral and textural space of any ensemble with which it is paired. As a result, the very *idea* of what is "orchestral" shifts. Rather than being defined as a particular grouping of instruments, it instead becomes the attribute of a particular vastness of sound. It makes it entirely possible to compose a symphony that will not necessarily use the symphony orchestra, so long as it advances a certain sense of form and sonic scope that seems in tune with examples from the repertoire. (A grand example is Ingram Marshall's *Fog Tropes* (1981), blending a brass sextet with the sound of Bay Area foghorns.)[4]

2) I mentioned sampler keyboards; along the same line is the entry of electronic instruments *as instruments* into the acoustic ensemble. The most obvious is the keyboard synthesizer, whose range of possible sounds is almost infinite now. Software design allows any fusion of sampled with purely synthesized sound, to the point now that this distinction is largely historical and no longer germane to current practice. *All* sound in the digital domain is increasingly fluid and blended. And it can become part of the orchestra (or any mixed ensemble) like any other instrument. John Adams has been particularly sensitive to these possibilities; I find his use of synthesizer in the second movement of his 1993 Violin Concerto to be convincing and magical. In a more radical manner, Paul Dresher

has for decades led a sextet that performs both his own work and that commissioned for him, and all the players use electronic instruments or digitally enhanced versions of acoustic ones.[5]

3) This leads to perhaps the greatest factor of all in the expansion of sonic potential, *processing*. The most simple and obvious form is amplification, and it's been resisted for a long time by those in the classical tradition. But the experience of listeners who have grown up with popular music standards is shaping the field. I realized this a couple of decades back, attending a Kronos Quartet concert in an intimate hall, where all four instruments were amplified (and for every piece, not just Crumb's *Black Angels*). In a sense it was unnecessary, but it *did* give the music a different visceral impact. As a result, there is a critical member of most ensembles now, along with those one sees onstage: the engineer who is running the mix. This goes back to the practice of Philip Glass and Steve Reich from their beginnings: in both cases the intent was to create a sound and an atmosphere more redolent of a rock concert as well as allow for the new balances between instruments that were previously impossible. (I think of the pulsating vocalises for Reich's singers in works such as the fourth movement of *Drumming* (1971) or *Music for 18 Musicians*.)[6]

4) And of course amplification is just the beginning. *Filtering* reshapes the timbral envelope of any sound (think John Lennon's voice in later Beatles songs). *Reverb* gives the reflective resonance we expect in good acoustic spaces. *Delay* multiplies a sound upon itself canonically. I've already mentioned Terry Riley; Ingram Marshall is also master of this in many of his pieces.

5) And there is yet one further step emerging: sounds that are synthesized, but combine aspects of both acoustic and electronic sounds into new fluid hybrids. The idea of *granular* synthesis is allowing composers to create increasingly present, realistic sounds that seem rooted in reality, yet in fact exist only in dream. These are not merely samples, but are sounds that can then be altered further and manipulated in a host of ways that before the restrictions of the sampled soundfile disallowed. (To take one of the simplest examples, your GPS "voice" is a synthesized sound that can read from a given text without having to assemble each word separately from a pre-existent sonic lexicon.)

6) These are just the tip of the timbral iceberg, but they do delineate the basic families of effects that have gained greatest common usage.

The upshot is that *all* these factors listed above become part of a spectrum of sonic stances from which a composer can choose and blend. The idea of *sound design*, originally related more to theater and film, is becoming a concept shaping concert composers' creative ideas and strategies. As I said before, it's a radically different idea of orchestration, and one vaster in sonority and richer in possible hybrids than ever before.

There is yet another creative zone: a zone between, inside, and outside of the studio and the concert environment. This one really has never existed before, and we are just starting to grapple with its possibilities and implications. It is the computer becoming an active partner in the compositional process.

The dream of artificial intelligence has always been seductive, and a subset of adventurous composers have worked from the outset of the digital era to find ways to "teach" computers to compose. Pioneers include Lejaren Hiller, James Tenney, and David Cope. Some efforts, like those of the last, have tried to define style-set rules to create "new" pieces in the language of Old Masters. For me, more convincing attempts tend to sound like nothing precedent.

The key is to find a balance between the two poles of algorithmic determinism and randomness. The latter is familiar to almost all readers, the former maybe less so. It posits a rule for transforming incoming information, which results in a specific product, usually more complex than the input. (One of the simplest strict algorithms in all music is the canon, which specifies a pitch interval of transposition and a duration of delay before the imitation begins; that's it, though it's not a guarantee of a *good* canon!) In the previous chapter I mentioned "generative music," which is largely an algorithmic product. And while patterns of motives can be spun into an endless textural wash with this method, it's important to realize that these rules can apply to any parameter of music (dynamic levels and envelopes, timbral components, orchestrational choices, textural density, etc.).

If the algorithm is strict, then it is a sort of conceptual "black box," and the piece is in fact a fixed entity like any other, *except* for the fact that the output may be the result of so many factors interacting that the creator can't conceive of the actual sound until she hears it. In that sense even the strictest construct results in music that is idiomatic to the computer. But the idea of *interactivity*—a kind of social bond between the human and the machine—has always had even greater sway over the field than a purely deterministic approach. As mentioned earlier, randomness (embodied in most programs as a random-number generator whose output can be assigned as values to any given range of any parameter) is a way to create permutation and unpredictability. The composer can still control the *degree* thereof, so that the "randomness bandwidth" inflects the piece to give it distinct character. (Though his visible output seems to have trailed off since the 1990s, Clarence Barlow is a composer who mined this vein with a series of very effective pieces suggesting a sort of extraterrestrial folk music and jazz. Another composer who creates astonishingly mutating processes that are more concerned with the morphing of one soundworld into another is Carl Stone.[7]) Or it can be tied to analysis of input from a live performer: by measuring it against particular parametric thresholds or "if-then" tests, different results can be generated, which will in turn elicit particular responses from the performer, and so on. The result is a sort of creative feedback loop that has a general character and structure common to repeated performances, but with great variety of detail from one to the next. (An early pioneer of this approach is Richard Teitelbaum; a more contemporary example is George Lewis.[8])

The program that comes the closest to this model, and increasingly comprises most of the others I've suggested so far, is Max. Because it is "object-oriented" (i.e., it contains smaller pre-coded programs that can be connected in a near-infinitude of ways, in a modular/graphic user environment), it has enormous power and flexibility. Its learning curve is not simple, but it provides results of exceptional sophistication that earlier could only be achieved by those who mastered an entire computer language. Its strengths are such that when the original company marketing the program folded, its user community united to save it under a new commercial rubric, and it has grown ever since like wildfire.

The implications of such an application to what I've called *openness* will be explored further on. It also creates an exceptional platform for cross-disciplinary *collaboration*, because its output values are essentially numeric, and applicable to any digitally controllable device (e.g., midi-instruments, audio processing units, lighting boards, and robots). Again Kyle Gann has a brilliant aphorism: "We may not have a common language, but we have common software." And I'll maintain that such software *is* making said language increasingly common and comprehensible from one community to another, ones that previously had no easy means to exchange their concerns and ways of thinking.

And as one further overarching observation, realize that *all* the innovations I've detailed so far can be blended in whatever mix desired. We are talking about a *spectrum* of applications, not a discrete series. This is a technical and conceptual "mash-up," and as all technology becomes increasingly and exclusively software-based, the ease of communication between applications themselves is growing daily. (An example is the fusion of Max with the sound-design program Ableton Live; the only problem with even mentioning such is that with the accelerating rate of change, any example I can provide may be outdated before this text even gets out to the world.)

All these startling innovations have occurred in the creative domain, the area of composition that is the *making* of new work. But there still remains one final realm to acknowledge, and this is the *context* in which art is made. It too is being altered, and this impact is perhaps the most radical of all. I'm naturally speaking of the information and communications revolution.

I came to some understanding of these shifting grounds a few years back at a "meet and greet" party for composers to the program where I teach. I asked an entering freshman what music he was interested in, and he immediately cited the piano music of Michael Finnissey. I would have been impressed with this erudition if it were coming from a doctoral student. Instead, it was from a seventeen-year-old. How could it be? Of course, by now the answer is so obvious I hesitate to even detail it. There are now so many online resources—YouTube, SoundCloud, Spotify, Naxos, and individual websites—constantly expanding their datasets and multiplying in number, that there really isn't any excuse now for not knowing *anything*. Indeed, more and more we are all expected to know *everything*. I spoke before of the instantaneous aural feedback that composition software provides. *This* feedback is similar, in that it enlarges exponentially the repertoire-knowledge field of composers at a critical stage in their development. Drastically different, seemingly conflicting pieces and aesthetics suddenly coexist. And that very simultaneity makes them seem ever less different or mutually exclusive to those encountering them for the first time.

I've been talking about information, but the development of communications represents just as seismic a shift. Today we think little of a video chat across continents via Skype or FaceTime. Yet for my generation, this is truly the stuff of science fiction rendered concrete and quotidian. The ability of composers not only to hear one another's work, almost in real time as it is created, but also to then contact one another, or for performers to do the same with composers, creates a contact-loop that is closer and faster, and yet also a net cast far wider. The implications for developing a career are obvious. Social media is now an essential tool for any young musician (and older ones too). Music can be self-published, recorded, and distributed. Though there are still very real reasons to have the third-party advocacy of certain "gate-keeping" individuals and organizations, the option of taking one's work directly to a plugged-in audience is a brave new world.

And these communications open up collaboration, not just in the way that artists in different media may find one another, but in the very idea of what a performance can be. We're not fully there yet, but the simultaneous performance based in multiple locations already has precedent, and the clarity of remote transmission will only grow greater, I suspect faster than we can even imagine. In fact, we're already at this point in mass media at the corporate level; all we need is for the technology to reach such a point of affordability that it becomes personal and not just institutional. The model is the personal computer, which escaped its corporate and university bonds, and became everyone's workstation, evermore powerful yet physically smaller.

For the past few decades there has been an insistent trumpeting of the change technology is bringing to music. I admit, the crusading zeal thereof at times seemed to me overdone, an excuse to justify superficial novelty at the expense of greater substance or to suggest short-cuts that ultimately could not make up for the hard-fought attainment of real craft. It's been a favored rallying cry of academic administrators, partly because it promised more efficiency and less employees. But I do think we have reached a critical mass, a genuine shift that's embodied in the Millennial generation. Technology provides the basis for a new "practicum" that any artist ignores at her peril. Of course not every development I've cited has to be utilized by any single composer, but he *must* understand his relation to them, in order to function successfully through the remainder of a career. Even more importantly, this technology provides the baseline for a whole concept of composition that is not only radical, but loops back to redefine and revivify the tradition that I don't believe has to be discarded. Some ideas of how this "reconnection" can occur will follow in upcoming chapters; ironically, it also emerges via technology's ties to more "futuristic" media and genres—sound art, performance art, installation, and open performative and collaborative action.

4

A Ringing in Our Ears

The greatest plaint from listeners about music of the twentieth century (one that continues to this day in somewhat debased form) is that music became confused and angry; it lost its sense of beauty and instead embraced ugliness; it justified any possible combination of sounds with intellectual excuses that had nothing to do with sound itself. And the musical means to effect this abduction from aesthetic truth and beauty were *dissonance, atonality, and serialism.*

This is a caricature, and I am going to stand against its worst cartoonish tendencies. Those three words are in fact quite different things and have been lazily conflated by a lot of commentary. So we need to parse them out carefully. But I also have to say there is a germ of truth in the critique. This chapter is concerned with how over the course of the later twentieth century an ideal of *harmony* has been allowed back in the arena. It is *not* a reactionary rant. Too much art from the modernist twentieth century has real, fresh truth and beauty embedded within that I can never deny, nor would want to lose. I am fully convinced what happened was necessary and for the best. But we *are* moving toward a new harmonic concept and practice, and I think it is one of the most important factors driving a "reintegration" of musical practices today. In order to reach this point of understanding, however, we will need more technical explanation than almost anywhere else in this text. This story has been told many times before, and any synopsis will be an oversimplification. But to set the stage, we must go back to the opening of the twentieth century and understand the context where music suddenly seemed to deny its roots. Though this text is not an analysis—it is ultimately a work of "creative criticism"—we still need some history and technical explanation. For some it will be old hat, and so you (who know who you are) can skip forward. For others it will be new. And even if it is familiar ground, some of my takes on the subject you may still find fresh. Before all else, though, we must define those three nasty words.

Dissonance has always been with us. Every new interval (the perceived difference/distance between two pitches) has always caused both concern and fascination when it first began to enter the vocabulary (like the mediant third in early-fifteenth-century *fauxbourdon*). Likewise, having intervals outside the accepted *consonances* (intervals derived from lower partials on the overtone series—to be explained in a moment) allowed the injection of tension into harmonic progressions (successions of chords). A dissonance was like a piquant sauce that added flavor; when it was *resolved* to a harmony that was more consonant, it was a little like the relief of drinking water after a bite of hot curry. Mozart even wrote a string quartet whose whole opening is a series of dissonances and carries that name as its subtitle. So this has been part of the language from the outset.

Arnold Schoenberg was a composer who always wanted to see the big picture in the development of music, and to be on the correct side of history. Before anyone rushes to knee-jerk judgment, it's important to acknowledge that his mastery of the great romantic practice of chromatic harmony at the end of the nineteenth century was real and virtuosic. Anyone who listens to *Verklärte Nacht* or *Gürrelider* (1899, 1901/11) and denies his craft needs to take his ears in for a tune-up. But Schoenberg felt that the increasingly fluid and frequent movement between different key areas, and the resultant incorporation of almost all the twelve chromatic tones (the white-and-black notes within an octave on the piano) into progressions, were unmooring music from its traditional tonal roots of key, scale, and triad. Eventually in 1905, halfway through his second string quartet, he threw away the key signature and wrote music that used the twelve tones expressively and intuitively. The music was far more motivically driven than before; harmonies tended to be byproducts of these compact thematic ideas than vice versa. Until about 1913, he wrote an extraordinary series of works we now call "free atonal" or "expressionist": the Op.11 and Op.19 piano pieces (1909, 1911), *Die Glückliche Hand, Das Buch der hängenden Gärten, Erwärtung*, and of course *Pierrot Lunaire* (1908/09, 1910/13, 1909, 1912, respectively). Personally, I still love this music. It's on fire, full of color and drama, whirling through ideas and sounds like an out-of-control kaleidoscope. And it's a perfect embodiment of the world of Central Europe, specifically Vienna, at the edge of the approaching precipice of the First World War.

Atonality perhaps is a misnomer. Even Schoenberg was skeptical that it was possible; his whole practice being deeply rooted in tonality from his first musical efforts. In his magisterial text *Harmonielehre* (Harmony Book),[1] he posited that dissonance was but the result of partials ever higher on the harmonic series becoming acceptable to musicians' ears, ultimately allowing the complete chromatic into musical discourse (there are those overtones again, the definition *is* just around the bend). So he still held onto a faith that at any moment in a work, no matter how fleeting, there was a hierarchy of pitches, relating to a foundation or center. It was "tonality," but just far more quicksilver than ever before.

Finally, *serialism* is Schoenberg's invention emerging in the 1920s, in fact the fruit of almost a decade of gestation and a sabbatical from composition, as he tried to figure out how the forces he felt he had unleashed could be tamed. He wanted the soundworld he had discovered to be subject to a new, comprehensive, and understandable set of rules that would renew harmonic practice for centuries to come, the way the "common practice" developed in the eighteenth century had flourished up till his youth. His solution was elegant—order the twelve pitches of the chromatic scale into a *series* (his term, rather than "row"), then derive its permutations using transposition (the same interval sequence starting from a different pitch), inversion (intervals up instead of down and vice versa), retrograde (reverse order of pitches in the series), and retrograde inversion (a combination of the last two). This gave forty-eight versions of the original. With it, he had enough to work with for the rest of his life.

There is no question that Schoenberg wrote a series of masterful pieces using serial technique, and many have been enormously influential. But for me (and I think for many) there is a serious flaw. The connection to tonal practice was more *symbolic* than *acoustic*. For example, Schoenberg would use a transposition of a row to the tritone (three whole-steps up, the symmetric dividing-point of the octave) as a substitute for the dominant (the chord and key area based on a perfect fifth above the tonic, a half-step greater than the tritone). This *seems* to function in the same way, and it's a recognizable event for those whose ears are attuned to notice it, but it doesn't really *sound* the same. His students Berg and Webern each wrote far more convincing serial works: Berg by structuring his rows to create references to earlier tonal practice (as in his Violin Concerto (1935), where the row allows a Bach chorale to seamlessly emerge as part of its melodic line); Webern by creating an abstract texture of motivic modules, usually in canon, that somehow sounds clearer and purer than almost anything before or since (his *Symphony* [1927–28] is a glimpse of a sort of serene non-tonal heaven). In short, Schoenberg's idea of serialism was more about idea than style, but in this case it was a fatal mistake.

We've already noted that composers in the postwar era took this technique and pushed it to its limits (citing Webern, incidentally, more than Schoenberg, Boulez being a prime example of this tactic). By applying serial techniques to other parameters such as duration, volume, articulation, and timbre, they developed a comprehensive approach that was called *total* or *integral* serialism. True, serialism had not been the only game in town. In the first half of the century, Bartók conceived an entire counter-practice that was wildly inventive in its rhythms; taut and rigorous in the way its motivically derived harmony interacted with invented modes. The post-Satie school *Les Six* created a uniquely French sound, straight from cafés on the boulevard. A host of highly individual "nationalists" created music that was fresh and dynamic, and far less self-conscious: Janacek, Nielsen, and Sibelius. And above all, Stravinsky and his followers promoted a neoclassical aesthetic that reimagined the common practice through a cubistically fracturing filter. But after the Second World War, these composers were either dead or increasingly ignored by the new generation. Stravinsky pulled off a great escape by himself embracing serialism in the 1950s (in a completely personal and frankly subversive way). Though integral serialism didn't last long, the "classic modernist" aesthetic underpinning it did, and European music became far more polemical and dogmatic, rather than genuinely revolutionary, than before.

The migration to the United States of so many influential European composers gave it an added jolt of credibility and influence on this side of the Atlantic. The more traditional American tonal practice never died out (after all, Ned Rorem is still with us, and remains a force), but the serial ideal *did* create a hurdle for any younger composer looking for establishment approval. American postwar modernism was not monolithic either, but it did view historical growth as a progressive line forward, similar to its European forebear.[2]

And yet an American countertradition, one quite forward-thinking, was already present. *Ultramodernism* was a term in use in the 1920s describing an American music that was radical but not as didactic (or homogeneous) as the European serial model. The leaders of the movement were Charles Ives, Carl Ruggles, Henry Cowell, Ruth Crawford Seeger, Dane Rudhyar, John Becker, Leo Ornstein, Wallingford Riegger, Joanna Beyer, and the theorist-scholar Charles Seeger. *This* music is in fact the source of what is increasingly called the "American Maverick" tradition. And though these composers were extremely different in their individual profiles and their musical concerns (as well as the sound of their respective pieces), I believe they remained more in touch with

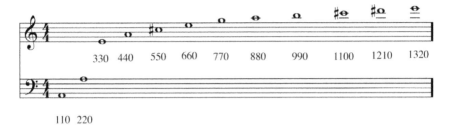

Figure 4.1 First twelve partials off A fundamental, with respective frequencies.

the whole issue of *sound* in a modernist framework than most of their European counterparts.

At last I can give that little mini-lecture on the harmonic series. (I realize that it is also called the overtone series *and* that overtones within it are also called partials. From this point on I will use the terms currently most accepted: harmonic series and partials, with the first partial being what's also called the "fundamental.")

Every sound we hear that is called *pitched* (with a distinctly identifiable rate of vibration called frequency—the A above middle C you hear when the orchestra tunes is 440 cycles per second) is in fact *the sum of a whole series of sympathetically vibrating pitches*. In fact, *every note is a chord*; those upper frequencies are the partials, and they are usually softer than the lowest tone, known as the fundamental. The varying mix and volumes of these partials creates the unique "color" of a sound, also known as its timbre.

The harmonic series is a dazzlingly clear and direct structure. Take any fundamental frequency, then multiply it successively by 2, 3, 4, 5, and so on. Each resultant frequency is the next partial. Every partial related by a multiple of 2 is an octave. Look at Chart 4.1.[3]

You see that when these frequencies are translated into the closest approximation to pitch letter-names, we begin to get something familiar. The first, third, and fifth partials spell out the root, fifth, and third of the major triad. The seventh partial is tuned slightly "off" from what we call our current "equal-tempered" scale (and yes, more on *that* to come in a moment), but still gives us the minor seventh that is the essential component of any dominant seventh chord. You'll also notice that there is a progressive "tightening" of the relationship between successive partials and their resultant pitches as one moves higher up the series. Every time we commence a new octave, there is more and more room for additional frequencies to exist within its boundaries.

This is an *acoustic reality*. Everything we hear that we call music comes down to some sort of correspondence (or lack thereof) with the harmonic series. Leonard Bernstein in his Harvard Norton Lectures, *The Unanswered Question*,[4] took at the time (1981) a controversial stand in advocating this as proof of tonality, due in part to that tonic triad emerging right at the beginning of the series. This was roundly criticized (especially because he used the linguistic theory of Noam Chomsky as a justification), but over time I think his instincts were correct. The harmonic series is *not* proof of the unquestioned superiority of common practice tonality (more precisely known as functional diatonic harmony). Rather, it is the more general rubric from which a whole family of harmonic practices can emerge. And this century is beginning to see a flowering and cross-pollination of several, some of which we'll explore here.

Back to the Ultramodernists—there are two composers who are particularly important to this story, Charles Ives and Henry Cowell. Ives, whose output is really so vast and ambitious that it's hard to pin him in any camp, created music that, on the one hand, was deeply connected to the world of popular song, Civil War marches, ragtime, folksongs, and hymn tunes from his remembered youth. What's evocative about it is that the source material being referenced is often buried and gradually exhumed during the course of the work (a process the foremost scholar of his music, Peter Burkholder, dubs "cumulative form").[5] Or it is framed by a gauzy mist of more chromatic music. In any case, there is a sense of the simple, haunting, naïve source, floating within a far more rich and complex sonic universe.

There is no specific proof that Ives rationalized the harmonic series into some sort of compositional system (though ironically, in *Chromâtimelôdtune* [1913–19],[6] he did create a proto-serial piece well before Schoenberg). But he was consistently interested in microtonality, composing a set of pieces for two pianos tuned a quarter-tone apart, and in his library was the classic acoustics text of Helmholtz, *On the Sensations of Tone, as a Theory for the Psychological Basis of Music*, which we must assume he had read.[7] His music *sounds* as though he had absorbed the lessons of the series.[8] In works such as the *Housatonic at Stockbridge* from *Three Places in New England* (1910–14), *From Hanover Square at the End of a Tragic Day the Voice of the People Again Arose* from the Second Orchestral Set (1909–19), and the outer movements of the Fourth Symphony (1912–26), one feels that cosmic forces are at work and that somehow all possible tones are vibrating sympathetically.[9]

Cowell, a California wunderkind from Bay Area bohemia, was a generation younger than Ives but a great friend and supporter. His signature use of piano clusters suggested an ideal of enriched harmony (in fact they are often precisely voiced, and their ranges chosen with evident care). But his great contribution is a work of extraordinary theoretical imagination, *New Musical Resources*.[10] Written in large part while still a teenager (though the influence of his mentor Charles Seeger is likely), it is an attempt to create a "unified field theory" of music that has yet to be equaled. Cowell makes the connection of frequency (speed of air pressure vibration), to rhythm (attacks of individual sounds in repetitive patterns), and to color (specific frequencies vibrating simultaneously in different ratios). All of these are in fact aspects of the same phenomenon, that is, *speed of repetition of an event*. Or another way of saying this is that on both micro- and macro-levels, in multiple parameters, all music is rhythmic. From this he began to expound a manner of composition, where harmonic series ratios could determine the pitches in a harmonic field, and the rhythmic patterns assigned to them. In one sense, it presages both integral serialism's attempt to apply the series to other parameters than pitch and the "time-point" system developed by Milton Babbitt. But unlike those, it was actually an extension from an initial *sound*. Cowell's ideas and his vision of a unified, "trans-parametric" practice remain a challenge and influential.[11] To take just one example, John Luther Adams has stated that his *Veils*, a six-hour electronic installation, is in fact an attempt to realize Cowell's suggested practice from the book.[12]

So from very early in the twentieth century, many American composers had considered the harmonic series as a source for their harmonic theory and practice. This was interrupted by serialism, but a few composers persevered in a very particular and American tangent of the approach, and I'll return to it soon. But first I need to make one general observation and then a brief trip to France.

The digression concerns the way that harmony is conceived and discussed in the twentieth century. The term itself is bandied about freely, but often without as much precision and scrupulousness as I would like. For many, post-tonal harmony basically means what happens when notes sound together, and nothing more. Indeed, when I was starting out as a composer, the term "simultaneity" was almost universal. It captured the sense of neutrality with which concurrent sounds were regarded, and it freed one from judgments of consonance versus dissonance. If one wanted to organize the coincident tones in some manner, fine: in that case what was aimed for was a particular *consistency* of pitch-groups, where their intervallic relationships could be discerned, and correspondences determined. The practice of *set theory* was the ideal embodiment of this attitude, teasing out exactly that sort of intervallic structure, with its differences and hidden similarities. And Elliott Carter in his *Harmony Book*,[13] a labor of decades, was able to derive on his own (and independently of Allen Forte, the theorist who "invented" set theory), his own version that covered exactly the same ground as Forte, and gave him a repertoire of pitch combinations he could draw from at any moment in a work.

Carter of course is most noted for his contributions to rhythmic practice, and his comprehensive explorations of metric modulation have bequeathed to us a technique that is applicable across the widest stylistic platform. His harmonic practice is also quite successful: one easily hears emphasis on certain intervals throughout a work, in particular in the way they may be associated with a specific instrumental line. It is *consistent and audible*, and as such completely successful. But I maintain—despite his obvious mastery in a series of undeniable works of genius and my own admiration for his work—that it's still not enough.

What's missing for me is *resonance*. And this is the aspect of "harmony" that goes beyond mere consistency to attain that aspect which I feel has always been its greatest strength: when pitches sound together, *the whole is greater than the sum of the parts*. There's no doubt that the modal underpinning and the repetition of minimalism achieves this often: John Adams's great wavelike orchestral textures are a grand example. Then how can I say Carter's harmony is audible but still lacking? It comes again to the difference between the symbolic and the visceral. Those consistent/predominant intervallic structures in his music *are* far more perceptible than, say, analogous structures in Babbitt. But what gives the music its momentum tends to be far more rhythmic and contrapuntal.

Resonance on the other hand involves reinforcement. Tones, if chosen correctly, placed in the proper registration (voicing), and orchestrated so as to create a timbral connection, can begin a sort of positive feedback loop. A technical term for this is "sympathetic vibration." Some of it is truly physical, and some of it is, I think, a psychological gloss we as humans place over sounds that approximate these relations. No matter what the scientific or phenomenological explanation, this feeling of sounds creating a *space* seemingly more vast than it should be, is perhaps the single most remarkable characteristic of harmony.

In the twentieth century, this harmonic aspect still comes through from composers not primarily concerned with it, almost despite themselves. I think of Stravinsky and Bartók, whose octatonic and synthetic-modal scales still created a hierarchy of pitches, which their musical instincts shaped into real resonance and progression. An even more convincing example is Messiaen,[14] whose modes again create a foundation to build on, but also whose experience as an organist was undoubtedly critical to his ability to build up rich, sonically "juicy" chords. Of postwar masters, Berio has always struck me similarly, maybe because he never really gave up on the voice and an underlying truth of folk song. From these examples, you may start to get my point, and internally hear the sonic quality I'm describing, and indeed advocating.

In the United States, a great tidal shift toward this sort of more open and inviting harmony began in the 1970s and 1980s, though as more of a return than a true reinvention. As a counterreaction to the serial/modernist paradigm, a number of composers re-embraced tonality in personal ways and became known as "postmodern."[15] George Rochberg was the first to gain renown (and notoriety) by foreswearing serialism. He had been one of the most prominent, and finest, composers in that idiom, but he felt upon the death of his son that it could not reach the expressive heights and depths he needed to reach, so he began to write a series of pieces that first collaged quotations from earlier repertoire (such as the 1965–69 *Music for the Magic Theater*), and then pastiches of original music, but written in deliberately anachronistic styles. The foremost of these are his Quartets No. 3–6 (1972–78; the latter three known as the "Concords"), and in particular the Third, which was a clarion call of return to a practice most had consigned to the dustbin.[16]

Four other composers advanced the cause in very different ways, in keeping with their divergent personalities. Jacob Druckman, though much more of the dramatic/colorist school (think Berio) nevertheless found the quotation of earlier music, especially early baroque opera, important to his aesthetic. A prime example is his appropriately titled piece *Windows* (which, as its title suggests, inserted fragments of earlier repertoire works into the orchestral fabric and won the Pulitzer Prize in 1972).[17] Also, by curating an influential series of festivals in the 1980s with the New York Philharmonic, he laid the groundwork for a way of discussing tonality again and created a "buzz" for postmodern musical experiment.

David Del Tredici took a highly personal route, by (like Rochberg) foreswearing early modernist success and writing a series of pieces based on *Alice in Wonderland*. These were highly dramatic, often hallucinogenic, even verging on psychic breakdown—very much in the spirit of its source, which has too often been sentimentalized and sanitized into a Victorian children's tale. They were also incredibly funny. His masterwork is *Final Alice* (1976), an hour-long monodrama for soprano and orchestra that sets the book's final chapter.[18] Along with consummate common practice technique and orchestration straight from

Richard Strauss, it also looped in on itself, got "stuck in grooves," and flew into psychedelic frenzies that could only have come from its contemporary context.

John Corigliano grew up in the bosom of classical music: his father was concertmaster of the New York Philharmonic. From early prodigious success he has carved out a body of work that, while relatively small, has created one of the finest and most seamless syntheses of contemporary techniques (in particular aleatoric, analogous to the later work of the Polish composer Witold Lutoslawski) with full-blooded romantic expression. His Symphony No.1 (1988; often called the "AIDS Symphony") is perhaps his finest and fullest expression of his aesthetic.[19] He also has written some of the most substantive and inventive of all film scores, and for a "classical" composer has won an Oscar, a feat nowadays almost impossible due to the corporatization and specialization of the field that once welcomed Copland.

Finally, William Bolcom, in part thanks to his daunting facility as a performer, having made a second career with his singer-wife Joan Morris, combined a thorough and intimate knowledge of the American popular song tradition with convincing mastery of dramatic expressionist orchestral writing, to create a blend that was similar to Rochberg's, but even more convincing when it embraced popular models. His *Songs of Innocence and Experience* (written over twenty-five years, premiered in 1984) is his unquestioned masterpiece, a setting of the complete eponymous Blake poems, which ranges from free-atonal expressionism to country and Western, to a triumphant reggae as its climactic conclusion.[20]

The music that all these composers represent was a necessary "cleansing" of ears conditioned to think music *had* to sound "modern" in a specific manner. They made the counterargument that if it was written in this moment, then by definition it was "contemporary." And each took the model of common practice harmony (and its entire toolbox of related techniques) and showed how it could still become the means of personal expression. They showed there were new tricks left for the old dog.

For some, this was enough; it proved the resilience of a music that came from basic intuition and practice, and was proof that composers don't have to think *too* much. But while I feel these works will stand the test of time, as a model for future growth they only go so far. While not reactionary, they are still *reactive*, in that the very act of refusing the dogmatic modernist paradigm was a sufficient advance. In a way, it cleared the decks to develop a truly twenty-first-century harmonic practice.

And now, as promised, we can take that hop across the pond. I was living in Paris in 1980–81, and I kept hearing about a composers' group called *L'Itinéraire* (yes, "The Itinerary"). The core members were Gérard Grisey, Tristan Murail, Hughes Dufourt, and Michel Lévinas. They had banded together in the 1970s, and saw an ancestor in Giacinto Scelsi, the great iconoclastic Italian composer whose most famous work was a series of etudes for chamber orchestra, each on a single pitch-class.[21] Boulez was very interested in their work, and had in fact anointed them as the "next thing."

And what was their thing? *Spectral music*, or for short *spectralism*; the name comes from "spectrum" and refers to the harmonic spectrum. This usually means the harmonic series, but in fact it more precisely means all frequencies bundled into any given sound, whether they fall in the series of not. The spectralists' approach was to take a given sound, often a brief recording, even of just a single note, and subject it to scientific analysis, in essence putting it under a microscope. Its separate components were teased out, studied, and then reconstructed into music for instruments, often blown up over a far greater timespan. A classic example is Grisey's *Partiels* (1975; from his eight-work 1974–86 cycle *Les Éspaces Acoustiques*).[22] It's derived from the recording of a single trombone note (E2). Yet it is orchestrated for eighteen musicians and lasts twenty-two minutes. It has a primal power; few recent composers have attained as "Beethovenian" a quality in their music.

While in Paris I attended 100 new music concerts in a single season, and kept a critical journal, recording my thoughts on all of them. I'm pleasantly surprised, even a little shocked on rereading it, of how little my initial reactions have changed. I wrote that the spectralists were a little like Debussy without the tunes. (Incidentally, Debussy, who was quite secretive about his working methods, may well have had a hand in the black arts of harmony as well; the whole-tone scale quickly emerges as one moves up the harmonic series—though that revelation is also a bit cherry-picked from the data.)[23] I still find justice in that judgment of mine, but it's of course a bit flip; these composers were after something different, and I didn't hear Grisey's landmark works during that year (and I feel he is the most important and influential composer of the group). In fact, spectralism emerged in an almost perfect historical "sweet spot."

Serialism's influence had waned, but the modernist idea of *construction* had not. And French music yearned for a way to assert itself in a manner that was freed from German influence but still embraced an idea of progress that came from modernism. Spectralism answered these needs. It was uniquely French, not only in a soundworld that was far more seductive (and even allowed octaves!) but also because a particular Gallic rationalism could be called into play in the precise analysis of sound-sources for a piece, and in the construction of the work based thereupon. It's not for nothing the greatest cathedrals of the Middle Ages are French; the ability to create a *resonant space* seems part of the genetic (or memetic) cultural code.

That rationalism also gave spectralism an edge. Many of its sounds *were* genuinely "beautiful," but beauty had been suspect ever since the end of the First World War, and by the end of the Second Great War, it was basically verboten. But spectralism's extremely scientific approach (replete with mathematical analysis of frequency relations) gave cover to composers entering this soundworld. It's a nasty and non-too-secret fact that composers, in their geekiness, get very excited, and indeed feel empowered, by the technical arcana of the field (in fact like most professions—look at doctors, lawyers, engineers, financial managers—why do artists have to be intuitive naïfs?). Spectralism answered this need with a vengeance. It allowed the French to reassert their intellectual, not just sensual, authority. It was a godsend. And it's not surprising either that like serialism, it too has migrated to the United States, first with the appointment of Murail to a teaching position at Columbia, more recently taken by his German counterpart Georg Friedrich Haas. Their new generation of students is in turn moving into influential teaching positions throughout the country.

Lest I start to sound too cynical here, I must emphasize that spectralism has a sound that feels acoustically rooted. It *does* seem connected to nature, to the world of sound as we actually experience it, rather than musical units being a code for a series of abstract symbolic relations (in fact, an analogy might be pursuable between serialism and analytic philosophy, with the increasing distance of each from real-world experience of their potential audiences). It also is highly professional, in that it understands the interaction between theory and practice, and the compromises that it demands. Since many of the pitch relations derived from spectral analysis do not fall into the traditional equal-tempered scale (that of the current piano keyboard), they need to be adjusted to fit the model. Much of the spectralist technique involves adjustments by microtones in individual parts, but without an overarching alternative tuning system that must be learned by all. This frankly makes the music much easier to perform. It *is*, as Baudrillard would say, a "simulacrum" of the real thing on which it's based, but it's close enough for rock-and-roll.

As such, spectralism is perhaps Europe's great gift back to the musical world, perhaps the other great revolution of the postwar era, along with minimalism. *The former creates a theory of harmony, the latter a theory of time.* Composers who find ways to combine these two great gifts, coming from the East and the West, have a good chance to write music that will meet the yearnings of listeners in the near future, with a music of space, freshness, and imagination.

But, as suggested before, this is not the end of the story. Back in America, there has been a countertradition of a "new harmony," and it has been gaining traction over decades and is starting to accelerate, in part thanks to technological innovation. Like the European version, it has its own technical armature of mathematics and theory, but in a way it is far more idealistic. You might call it a *retuning* of music itself.

Time for another mini-lecture, but we now have enough background to handle it. Our piano has sounded the way it now does only from the early- to mid-nineteenth century. The tuning that emerged then is called "equal temperament," and it ensures that every "named" pitch-class (C, C#, D, etc.) is related by a pure octave in every register (a ratio of 2:1 in frequency from one to the next above). Likewise, every adjacent pitch (white to black, except B-C and E-F) is also an equal interval, known as a semitone or half-step. This system is the result of a series of choices that emerged from the increasing importance of keyboard instruments and a desire for some practical musical results, above all equally balanced transitions from one key to another, called modulations in tonal music.

But something very real is also lost in the process. All the other intervals are compromised. As soon as one tries to get one type of interval as pure and "perfect" as possible (such as the 3:2 perfect fifth or 5:4 major third), others become less so. It's a bit "hall-of-mirrors meets down-the-rabbit-hole." If one chooses to tune certain categories of intervals other than the octave and semitone to the exact ratio they exhibit on the harmonic series, an enormously rich and exotic soundworld emerges, and it *does* have its own logic, in fact a very rigorous mathematical basis. A vast array of intonational (tuning) possibilities opens up; it's like moving from a 2-D world to 3-D, or even more dimensions. And in the process, composers who choose to pursue this route (often called "just intonation" for the emphasis on "just" or pure intervals) feel they are moving toward something far more "natural" and essential to the nature of sound itself. Certainly, this lines up with the theories of Pythagoras, the great-granddaddy of all intonational theory.

The American composer who first went out fully on this limb was the great iconoclast Harry Partch. His life was often that of a hobo or squatter until late in life, when his work began to be recognized by academia and he was invited to university residencies. He designed all his own instruments, most of them percussion, tuned to a forty-three-tone-to-the-octave scale that gave just intervals of the third and fifth, justly tuned up to the eleventh partial. His book *Genesis of a Music* begins with the claim that "all music written since the Greeks has been a lie," and then proceeds to outline the counterargument in almost 500 pages dense with equations.[24] The music is propulsive, funny, almost drunk on sound, and definitely "corporeal," to cite one of the composer's favorite words.

Partch's student Ben Johnston (1926–2019) has taken perhaps the most courageous path imaginable of any twentieth-century composer. Partch's instruments opened up a wild new sonic realm, but most of them, being percussion, were not retunable (or if so, not quickly). As a result, the music has a fixed harmonic quality, and it is rhythm that gives the music its momentum. Johnston took on the herculean task of developing a comprehensive system and its notation that allows musicians on any traditional instrument to perform in just intonation. (The drawback of course is that there is a very long learning curve, both conceptual and aural.) He also enlarged the original Partchian paradigm so as to allow the system to tune to perfect intervals that emerge anywhere on the series. His most famous piece is his fourth string quartet (1973), a virtuosic demonstration that takes the hymn "Amazing Grace" and moves from Pythagorean tuning (pure fifths only), through just tuning of thirds and fifths, to purely tuned intervals derived from the seventh partial. His entire quartet cycle is not just extraordinary in its craft and imagination but also pulls off Johnston's stated goal, the re-imagining of Western classical music as though just intonation had become the standard instead of equal temperament.[25]

These are not the only examples of the approach. Lou Harrison, a friend of seemingly almost every composer in his lifetime (e.g., he arranged the performance of Ives's Third Symphony that won the composer his belated Pulitzer Prize), used just intonation throughout his career as part of his overall technical package, in large part because of his devotion to non-Western music, in particular Indonesian, Chinese, and Korean. Of the founding minimalists, La Monte Young has taken the approach to a very personal and extreme limit, retuning the piano so as to perform an immense meditative opus titled *The Well-Tuned Piano* (1961–87, continuing), which like a raga is a structure that, while consistent in its overall structure and direction over its six-hour span, is also open to his improvisational fancy. Here the aim is much more explicitly spiritual and contemplative. The tuning is designed to create an aura of sympathetically vibrating strings that in turn create clouds of overtones. In the texture one starts to hear ghostly overtone melodies in the upper registers; it's rather like angels dancing. Young has always remained an outlier, albeit enormously influential. He's had significant patronage that allowed him to set up a permanent installation space in New York with his wife the light-artist Marian Zazeela: the "Dream House," where most of his performances occur. His disciple Michael Harrison currently seems to be performing a function somewhat like Johnston to Partch, taking the principles of his teacher into application by increasingly varied ensembles, both instrumental and vocal.[26]

And so here we stand well into of the new millennium. From a variety of sources—postmodern "returning-tonality," European spectralism, and American "precise tuning" (a marvelous portmanteau word of John Luther Adams that covers the plethora of approaches embodied in non-equal temperament intonation)—there is now a range of approaches and attitudes toward harmony to suit a dizzying range of composers. All of them get down to one essence—there is an *acoustic reality* immanent in the harmonic series that we all ignore at our peril. There is no single path here, but unless composers accept just how *real* sound is to listeners, with its resultant possibilities and constraints, there will always be a danger of a disconnect between creator and audience. For me, there are grounds for hope. In every musical culture that moved to a level of extraordinary abstract experimentation, there has been a return to understanding that sound enters into the human ear, which has specific mechanisms for processing it. Cowell I think had it right: the divisions between color, pitch, and rhythm are artificial. Harmony, timbre, and rhythm are alternate manifestations of the same thing, the thing that gets into our blood. The intervention of the mind can of course shape what is heard, but how much better to have a fruitful dialogue between the physiological and the cerebral than to let only one or the other dictate how we experience art. That dance between brain and ear is returning to a necessary balance.

Open the Window

A few years ago I finally visited the Maverick recital hall near Woodstock, New York. It's a rustic, weathered "music shed," a type which dots the Northeast, and has inspired similar summer concert spaces throughout the nation. While a renowned concert venue for decades, it has one particular historical distinction. It was here, on August 29, 1952, that John Cage's *4'33"* was premiered. This is of course the famous "silent piece," a work for piano in three movements, where in each the performer closes the keyboard for a specific amount of time (the official timings are 30", 2'23", and 1'40", the total being the title), raising it between movements. David Tudor was at the keyboard, and it was a delicious irony, since he was unquestionably the era's greatest virtuoso performer of insanely difficult new music. For Cage to ask him to do *nothing* was in itself a great act of chutzpah. But of course, the piece was much, much more. One can easily imagine the hall's side windows open to let in the cooling summer breezes, and sounds from outside drifting in; as it began to dawn on the audience what was happening, their own sounds of confusion and discomfort began to mingle with those from nature. Cage repeatedly said this was his favorite work of his output, and he was not teasing. It realized his aesthetic more succinctly than any other piece.[1] And it invented a new art form.

This chapter deals with noise. I'm not speaking about sounds that annoy, distract, or even harm us, the colloquial definition of the term. Rather I'm speaking from the scientific definition, that is, of sound that does not possess a regularly, consistently repeating frequency and waveform. *That* is a definition based on the presence or absence of steady, identifiable pitch and color. The more these are present, the more *musical* it seems to us. If it isn't a tone that we can sing back easily, it's noise.

Noise on the whole has been kept out of the concert tradition. There are a few outliers, essentially novelty pieces, such as the cannons in Beethoven's *Wellington's Victory* and Tchaikovsky's *1812 Overture*. But sounds from outside the pitch spectrum have tended to be mimicked by instruments, "tamed" and brought into the acceptable melodic/harmonic framework. The noise is a memesis of something already in the environment, a symbol to be incorporated into some sort of narrative. Only in the twentieth century do we start to have instances of composers who actively seek to bring "real" noise into their concert pieces. I've mentioned already the Italian Futurists, George Antheil, and Edgard Varèse (the latter being by far the most important, with his elevation of unpitched percussion to equality with the other orchestral instruments, above all in *Ionisation*, one of the first works exclusively for percussion ensemble[2]). Once again, we need to examine the origins, to follow the historical thread. Trust me, it all leads to our present moment, and we're richer in our ability to make critical judgments for the knowledge such background imparts.

Right after the Second World War, concomitant with the invention of the tape recorder, the practice of *musique concrète* emerged. Its premise was the culling of sounds from the world, and their rearrangement into works where previously unheard, impossible relations between them emerged. It being a largely French movement, there was a strong emphasis on abstraction and an avoidance of any too-obvious referentiality. Purity was the name of the game, no matter how diverse the original sources.[3]

So the window was already open when Cage appeared. But what he did forever changed the conceptual framework for how any musician or listener dealt with the spectrum of sounds. First, he simply *accepted* all sounds as possible and equal for use in an artwork. Second, he pushed that acceptance to an extreme by allowing *chance* to determine which sounds to use. And third, in the process he invented a new art form.

Cage always saw himself first and foremost as a composer (even though he also showed definite genius as a visual artist throughout his career). And so, when in the very first essay of his debut writings collection *Silence*, he stated that "all music is organized sound,"[4] it had a radical ring, in that it emphasized *sound*, unbiased as toward its source. But Cage also used the term "music," and was clear that he was still thinking about a discipline that had never been challenged on its own turf. Indeed, Cage's dictum has continued to guide the infiltration of the concert music tradition with sounds ever-further from the acceptable pitched spectrum. In Europe at this moment, perhaps the most radically influential composer is Helmut Lachenmann, who has invented and carefully notated an entire catalogue of sounds produced by acoustic instruments, which artfully avoids their "normal" means of production. It's too simple to say that all his pieces use only "noise" in their writing, but its presence does give them an extraordinarily unique character. And strange to say, when listening carefully, in a sense "through" the sounds, one actually begins to hear formal strategies such as sonata and variations, a timeless ground upon which this new field is flowering.[5] In this sense Lachenmann is similar to Schoenberg, who wanted to renew the tradition with his innovations. As the latter "emancipated the dissonance," so the former has now "emancipated noise." In the European vision of aesthetic development, it is evidence of progress, of yet another frontier opened for exploration. There's life yet in the old horse.

But Cage was to open up something even bigger. Despite his understanding of his work as music, he was open to the fact that it would open the doors to a whole new range of creative minds and spirits. And just as he, a composer, would make visual art, so those not trained as musicians could make *sound art*.

And sound art is exactly what has since emerged. Cage himself helpfully showed the way with a series of works: the great cocktail party cacophony of *Variations IV* (1963) mixed live chatter with classical repertoire in an exotic sonic fruit salad; half of *Score: Forty Drawings by Thoreau* (1978) is made of delicate wisps of instrumental sound, followed by almost exactly the same amount of time that was then taken up with a recording of dawn at Stony Point, NY; Cage's own reworkings of Joyce into "mesostics" in his live solo performances took words into the realm of pure sound—a medium that was somewhere between music, theater, and poetry; and the creation of an entire work from the sound of amplified touching and scraping of branches and cacti in *Child of Tree* (1975).[6]

If anyone could make art with sound, it was going to be something quite different from what it had been only when musicians were making it. And so sound art has in fact developed on parallel paths, depending on whether it is made by musically trained or visually trained artists. The former (composers) tend to view sound as a medium that will be structured in an architecture that suggests a pattern of relationships, as does abstract music. The resultant forms may be radical, an arrangement never before conceived, but they are "formal" nonetheless. The latter (artists) can see sounds as far more metaphoric and symbolic of different cultural issues; from a different angle, they can be extremely visceral in their response, allowing sounds to exist and develop with very little further intervention.[7]

This division is of course not hard-and-fast. In truth, all sound art now exists on a continuum that is subtly gradated. Perhaps the single greatest determinant of art being given this name is that it occurs in a museum or exhibition space, rather than a concert venue. But though this economic/sociological distinction may be the simplest and the cleanest, nevertheless there *are* differences of approach to the discipline, depending on the artists' backgrounds.[8]

Let me take two examples. In the composer corner we have John Luther Adams. I've already mentioned *The Place Where You Go to Listen*. In one sense, it isn't sound art at all, as all its sounds are in fact synthesized, arranged to respond to the trigger of incoming data. But in its installation format, the piece is very much aligned with museum practice (and actually it exists only in a museum). In fact, it is an *environment*, open-ended, never the same on any day or time, a mirror of the world, but one that hasn't existed until now. Rather than *follow* its development, we *observe* it. We come and go as we please, and our role as an audience is freed of any concert etiquette or expectations.[9]

On the artist's side we have Janet Cardiff. A Canadian sound artist, her reputation was founded on a series of "artist walks," using a personal blend of conceptual, performance, and soundart elements. Each listener was a unique audience; s/he would be given a portable playback device with a prerecorded soundtrack. On it Cardiff, with her seductively deadpan voice, narrated the walk through a prescribed route, rather like a tour guide. But elements of narrative, history, and fiction became intertwined, supplemented by archival documents given the participant at the start, which the listener viewed only when told by the artist. I took one of these through Central Park (*Her Long Black Hair*, 2004), and one wonderful byproduct was that as one passed a site like the zoo, one heard animal noises both on tape through the headset and live from outside, and it became almost impossible to distinguish which was which. Thus, one's listening acuity was stimulated and attention enhanced.

Cardiff represents perhaps the majority of artists working today, in that she doesn't fall into a single easily categorized medium. Another piece I've experienced is very much an object, an old library card catalogue, in which was embedded a tiny sound system for each drawer (*The Cabinet of Curiousness*, 2010). When one opened any single one, a soundclip (which could be musical, ambient, vocal) played. A participant could open any number and mix of drawers to assemble a piece of sorts. The use of an obsolete object with associations of memory and archiving, combined with the ineffable quality of its emergent sounds, was gently humorous and haunting.

It's clear from the description above that such a piece is very much open-ended, and an installation. But Cardiff also has created pieces that come closer to a musical formal model. She has collaborated on several with her composer husband George Bures Miller, and these tend to have more of a fixed arc such as *The Murder of Crows (2008)*. I admit I'm not quite as taken with them; they seem a little like mini-operas without live agents. But they do fill a space between the cracks of different media. Working with a fixed musical object, however, Cardiff has created a piece that is her signature, *40-Voice Motet* (2001). This takes the sixteenth-century work *Spem in Aulium* by the English renaissance composer Thomas Tallis and assigns each voice to a separate loudspeaker. They are arranged in a circle, and each is small enough to take on a slightly anthropomorphic air, a head on a spindly torso.[10]

Many musicians, and in particular musicologists, will say what's the big deal? The music is a masterwork and already well-known, albeit in a rarefied repertoire; so to some it will seem cheap of Cardiff to appropriate it (and indeed, many people experiencing the piece unfortunately may come away with little or no awareness of Tallis's existence). But these criticisms miss what is remarkable about the piece. The fact that each voice has been recorded to a separate track allows a sort of interior aural exploration of the piece that has never before been possible. Not even a singer in the choir has ever had such an experience; it is both completely individual *and* global, thanks to the technology. And since in its installation format the piece plays as a loop (each cycle presaged by a few minutes of the recorded preparations and banter of the choristers), listeners can enter and leave as they please, and listen as many times as they want. Having now experienced it several times in different venues, I have noted that for probably a majority of listeners, it is a deeply contemplative experience, one that, perhaps unfairly, they would never have if they encountered the work in a concert hall.

Sound art is in its infancy. More and more young artists are seeing it as a viable part or even as a concentration of their practice. Its range of potential realizations is vast. It can be performative, purely acoustic (think of increasing numbers of "sound walks" being offered as forms of Oliverosian "deep listening"), or it can be entirely prerecorded (the river soundscapes of Annea Lockwood for instance). Or it can be a fertile mix of the two, with a highly interactive flavor.

Increasing numbers of young composers see installation/ambient work as a natural part of their creative spectrum. (Recently, I have seen a focus of interest on Ashley Fure, whose work combines aspects of controlled noise, installation, and theater into products that push the traditional limits of opera.) It's clear that a new factor in the making of aural art is emerging, and I call it *sonic essentialism*. By this I mean that a deep investigation and understanding of sound, unbiased by its source or internal components, becomes the basis of new art, which though experienced in time, often has a very different experience *of time.* The second word of the term comes from the idea of "essences," of what is "essential," a base of absolute zero. This attitude now runs across an increasingly wide stylistic gamut. This stance underlies the sort of audio analysis at the basis of spectral practice just as much as for the most radical noise-based free improvisation or an ambient gallery installation. In a sense, as the spectrum of possible sounds for aesthetic use expands, all music in a sense becomes sound art. Cage, whose near-silent laugh was iconic, infectious, and a form of sound-art performance in its own right, has more reason than ever to be pleased.

A Bigger Playground

I've made several references to "openness" as an emerging characteristic of new music, in fact perhaps *the* distinguishing one for the coming era. As its very name implies, though, it's quite vast and varied in the ways that it can be invoked and applied. And so, in hopes of clearing away some ambiguity, this chapter attempts to parse out the concept into several different manifestations. Once we have them all in view, maybe then we can start to see how they connect to provide a conceptual umbrella within which a new practice is growing.

At the very start, I'd like to connect openness to *multiplicity*. For centuries, we've tended to think of a work of art as unique and immutable. That is, there is only one of any work that bears a particular title/name, and that work remains the same whenever we encounter it. In the visual arts, the work in question has tended to be a painting or sculpture. In literature, it is a text that is a novel, essay, or poem. In the classical tradition, it is a piece defined by a score, whose notation fixes the result so that it is unchanging with each new performance. (Admittedly, *interpretation* allows for divergence of tempo, rubato, phrasing, etc., in the service of expression, but the basic arrangement of notes and durations is the one thing that cannot be varied.)

But throughout the twentieth century, the definition of a "piece" has expanded to become either a set of instructions for realization or a set of variables that can form different combinations. In either case, this piece involves choice on the part of performers and variation in the final result from one execution to another. This certainly is not new; I've mentioned the cadenza in classical practice, and of course there is jazz, which we'll return to later. In the immediate aftermath of the Second World War, a genuine movement of open-form works emerged. Some of them involved a "constellation" or "mobile" form, where the elements were not privileged to have a specific order. Many of Cage's "Happening" pieces of the 1960s (with *HPSCHD* [1969] being perhaps the ultimate) set loose a world of events with varying degrees of connection or cross-reference, unconcerned with the ultimate formal flow or shape. (Indeed, they not only often denied teleology, but the very idea of sequence; simultaneities of their elements could appear in unpredictable degrees of density.) Earle Brown's *Available Forms* series (1 and 2, 1961–62) takes a slightly more craftsmanly approach, and remains one of the most successful manifestations. Even Boulez and Stockhausen explored the concept, the former in his never-completed Third Piano Sonata (1955–63), the latter in works such as *Zyklus* (1959) for solo percussion (while it did have a fixed order, the work's literally circular form meant it could start at any point in its cycle and end immediately before that point).[1]

Composers also explored greater *indeterminacy*, that is the deliberate presentation of ambiguous information or situations that would necessitate a creative response from the performer to complete the piece. In this sense the player became a type of co-composer. Graphic notation was one means to this end, though not the only. And again, Cage was a leader, for example, creating works such as *Music Walk* (1958), in which multicolored graphic images on transparencies could be overlaid to create a score that the performer would then learn according to her own "rules" for interpretation of the notation. In some indeterminate works this could require as much practice as the most difficult traditionally notated piece; in other cases, a spontaneous improvisatory response would be demanded.[2] As one sees, the underlying strategies were widely varying, but the basic principles of freedom of choice and variation of result remained constant.

In the mid-twentieth century, these approaches could be controversial, and also more easily dismissed. Critical commentary could marginalize them, placing them on the "experimental" end of the spectrum. Many composers regarded them as "cheating," relinquishing the responsibility of the composer for every event in the score she created. Ironically, this attitude may have been in part a guilty byproduct of the exceptional specialization of composers at that time, when fewer and fewer had backgrounds as serious performers. Now I find a completely fixed score by a younger composer more of the exception than the rule. There are "conservative" models now that incorporate aleatoric elements, ranging from Lutoslawski to Corigliano. But more importantly, the vast majority of younger composers have a performance background again, though it tends to be in rock (or in fewer cases, jazz) rather than classical. And of course these traditions have improvisation at their core. So the idea of leaving some choice to a performer doesn't seem alien at all.

Further, though by no means exclusively so, this attitude strikes me as quite American, in that an idealistic part of the national ethos is democratic, trusting the instincts of the individual to make the right decision in service to the community. Many composers now don't want to be dictators. The hierarchical structure of orchestras, with their master-leader conductors, is suspect. And the responsibility of the composer shifts; it becomes one of a director, one who creates a situation *of structured freedom*. There is still enormous craft and ingenuity involved; the constraints, directions, and notations in a freer context need to be skillfully conceived and communicated in a manner that elicits an expressive and focused result. There will still be composers who evidence greater or lesser skill, as they take up this challenge. For example, one of the most striking proofs that such quality can be maintained in an open environment was a *Sonic Meditation* I heard more than two decades ago, directed by Pauline Oliveros in New York's Cathedral of St. John the Divine. She told the audience she would begin to play the accordion, then that each listener would respond to what they heard by singing a tone. She then added that everyone was directed to listen next for the *most distant* sound they could hear in the crowd (which was well over a thousand) and respond to *it* when they sensed a change of pitch. That one element of "distant" listening changed everything; soon there were huge chordal waves sweeping over the audience with tidal force. The genius was in the scrupulous crafting of the instruction.

A more tangential result of this open form is a new sense of *spaciousness* that has emerged in pieces. This comes in part from the weakening of directionality (teleology) in pieces with more open, "loosened" form. If a work becomes more like an installation or mobile in its effect (whether it is actually so or not in its technique), our own expectations become concomitantly relaxed. Obviously more theatrical works can take on these new temporal dimensions if the dramatic pacing suggests it—the operas of Philip Glass are the prime exhibit here. But even more germane I think are the increasingly vast aural landscapes of Morton Feldman (as we first remarked upon in Chapter 3). He played, in a curious sense, Berg to Cage's Schoenberg. By that I mean Feldman adopted many key aspects of Cage's aesthetic and technique, but he never could deny his ear's taste in the almost puritanical way that his mentor promoted. Feldman made a number of provocative and influential works in the 1950s and early 1960s that allowed performer choice within a graphic framework (in this case literally, as a Cartesian matrix with registers blocked out, within which one could choose notes). But he ultimately abandoned the approach. The fact was, he had an extraordinary ear for carefully shaped, slowly evolving harmony, albeit nontonal. His chords were more like beautiful sound-blocks that cycled and subtly mutated; the governing principles were actually not far from those of Varèse, except that the resultant sound couldn't have been more different. So almost despite himself, Feldman created a new *beauty*, pure and abstract like that of his contemporary painter colleagues and friends, yet at the same time supremely sensuous. And it demanded to be savored and lingered over, which led to ever-greater durations, culminating in his six-hour-long second string quartet. Feldman himself said that his work moved from the realm of duration to that of *scale* and that definition feels right; listening to one of these pieces is like a long journey by car where the landscape gradually changes before you over hours.[3] It's rich in detail but also iconic in character. It changes at a pace that is not noticeable until one reflects on where one has been. One can't help but feel that Feldman's early engagement with music that refused to impose limits on its parameters helped to free his imagination to eventually write completely notated music that was limitless in a different manner.

And for a final thought on openness/space in relation within the musical work before moving to a larger context, we need briefly to return to Cage's gift of the idea of *silence*. He spoke of music's primal elements being sound and silence, and it does seem that now composers are just beginning to take up the challenge for how to articulate and structure the latter. I once heard the composer Lisa Coons make a remark in a lecture that what we needed now was a "taxonomy of silence." Silence may not be the blank slate we've always thought it was. It may have different "resonances," depending on the context of its appearance, the space in which it occurs, the psychology created for its conception. At present the leading exponent of this approach is the *Wandelweiser* group, which is based primarily in Europe, but has a prominent member in the American composer Michael Pisaro, who often creates subtle and ineffable mixes of field recordings with sine tones and live instruments. The Swiss composer Jürg Frey has written piano pieces whose sparseness makes each note seem an event on the scale of a phrase or even section of a piece (one note or chord at a time, in a single line; no counterpoint). All of these composers are searching for an intersection of the rhythms and spaces of nature with musical discourse. It's a brave new world, and I suspect one that, like minimalism, will create suspicion and skepticism because of what's "not there," but which I also feel with time will start to reveal valid and tangible avenues of technical, expressive, and aesthetic exploration.[4]

Another form of openness is an increasing sympathy for influences from extramusical disciplines. I call it *cross-disciplinary pollination*. Historically, composers have of course been influenced by and responded to nature; they have set literary texts, both prose and poetry; they have celebrated important historical and cultural events. But a compositional practice based on the actual *practice* of another discipline is far more rare. In fact it seems to be a specifically twentieth-century approach. Perhaps the greatest single example is Iannis Xenakis. Trained as an architect (he was in fact Le Corbusier's assistant and did most of the design work for the famous Philips Pavilion at the 1958 Brussels World Fair, a structure that also housed Varèse's *Poème Électronique*), Xenakis is best known for his development of "stochastic music," which is governed by probability theory. And while written out like fully notated scores, his pieces are in fact the product of a set of algorithmic constraints defining the "edges" of a work that are filled in by the process's own "controlled-randomness" decision-making. In this sense they too have elements of the aleatoric and indeterminate. (I also think of them, due to their modeling on natural phenomena, as predictive of the emergence of chaos theory.)

But just as important as are the elements of scientific method, mathematical discipline, and information theory, the influence of architecture is critical to Xenakis's work.[5] He too is a composer who creates a different sense of musical space from what we've known before. It can be as vast as Feldman's (though not as temporally long); the main difference is that it is far denser in information and more violent and aggressive in character. A work such as *Jonchiaes* (1977) for orchestra is a hurricane, a rockslide, a tsunami: choose your metaphor.[6] Xenakis's Greek heritage comes to the fore in a unique combination of Homeric violence with Aristotelian rationality.

There are two important aspects of the composer's architectural stance. One is the actual work process: a general idea would often elicit a sketch in a purely graphic mode; this in turn would be translated into a precise but abstract visual rendering of the musical elements (pitch, duration, volume, timbre), rather like a blueprint. Finally *this* version would be translated one final time into musical notation. The analog to a flow from sketch to blueprint to maquette is obvious.[7]

The other architectural aspect of Xenakis is the most obvious of all: throughout his career he created a series of structures in which to present music that was specially designed for the space. These (known as *Polytopes*) were multimedia/multisensory environments, incorporating groundbreaking computer-controlled lighting systems and sophisticated spatial sound diffusion.

One of the composer's greatest electroacoustic works, *La Légende D'Er* (1977), was designed for the Polytope constructed on the Beaubourg plaza in Paris, and one can only imagine (since we do not have video or film of the interior) what the impact would have been on those who entered the maelstrom.[8] Another form of openness has already been suggested in some of the examples before, but now should be cited conclusively, *technological interactivity*. We have seen the idea that a composer can create some sort of system or set of relations that is set into action. The mutual effect of elements within begins to create the resultant piece. The terms "algorithmic" and "generative" are already in play. But the technology is moving at such a rate that these sonically self-perpetuating systems are easier to define and activate than ever. Max is one of the key elements of this movement. But it's again worth acknowledging ancestors. In retrospect, David Tudor stands out as we get more access to a recorded archive that until recently was relatively hidden. We have earlier encountered him as the premiere performer of *4'33"*, but aside from his own pianistic virtuosity, he was a constant collaborator with Cage throughout both of their lives, giving up the piano in the 1960s and devoting his energy to live electronic music, most of it in scores for Merce Cunningham's dance company. Tudor created networks of electronic circuitry that began to generate feedback effects that he then "rode" a little like a bucking bronco. *Toneburst* (1975) is like a construction site, full of noise and unstoppable energy. Its sonority is orchestral in scope, even though it has nothing to do with "musical" sound as traditionally defined (and note here the connection to sonic essentialism). While his work began with analog technology, his use was completely different from most composers working with analog synthesizers at the time, and is predictive of computer-driven algorithms (which he in fact moved to as the software caught up with his vision).[9]

And finally, it's important to realize that this approach is hardly restricted to a hermetic avant-garde universe. The very term "ambient music" was coined by the composer-producer Brian Eno, who also has made "generative music" part of the lexicon. Eno often works with the basic studio tools of editing and processing, rather than the sort of formal algorithms one can construct in Max. But just as Cage's use of chance procedures undermined the authority of serialism's technocratic method, so Eno's ambient landscapes show how far simpler technology, combined a proper *attitude*, can go to create hypnotic and alluring art. Sophistication comes in many forms.[10]

Much of what we've discussed so far concerns multiplicity, freedom, and space of the *conceptual* sphere in which a work is created. But just as important is the interaction of different disciplines in the *performative* realm. Composers who combine a variety of performance disciplines in their own work are nothing new, and indeed the virtuoso who created an audience for his music by means of his performance mastery is a familiar type throughout history: Vivaldi, Liszt, Chopin, and Paganini to name but a few. As the twentieth century progressed, however, composers became more specialized and performed less in public. Part of this was due to a parallel specialization of performers, who became so advanced that many competent composer-performers gave up trying to compete with them: they started to look amateurish in the public's eyes, even if their musicality was still deep and musicianship real. And also technology played an increasing role in this divide. Recordings made it easier for a composer to preserve and present work in alternative formats than the live concert. And once the computer entered the equation, it was possible for a composer to conceive, write, and hear at least a mockup of a piece from beginning to end, all without the mediation of performers. (And indeed some composers embraced the possibility of this closed loop, creating music entirely within the recorded realm.[11]) In short, the performing composer was a dwindling presence in the late twentieth century. Fortunately for the art, though, s/he has made a comeback. There are increasing numbers of highly professional composer-performers now. Not surprisingly, many are pianists, such as John McDonald, Eric Moe, and Amy Williams. And perhaps the premiere example comes from an earlier generation (though still with us) of Frederic Rzewski (more on him to come). But we see singers entering the field as well—for example, Lisa Bielawa, Kate Soper, and Caroline Shaw. Their presence and success prove a point; that is, that no matter what they do on stage, audiences *want* to see a composer in some performance role. Both Steve Reich and Philip Glass understood this from the outset of their careers, performing with their own ensembles, even if the parts they played may not have been the most difficult in the group. This act of joining the musicians bespeaks a certain solidarity with them; it reassures the audience that the composer is willing to share the risk of her piece publicly, and it lends a greater authenticity to its presentation.

But I am thinking beyond this paradigm, welcome and important as it is. I'm thinking about a performance practice that actually blends different time-art disciplines into a new synthesis. Of course, we have had various forms of music theater with us from antiquity on, and opera is the natural example of such a synthesis, now with four centuries of development and repertoire. But Harry Partch was an early American advocate for pushing this synthesis both further forward *and* backward, seeing his pieces as spectacles reviving the tradition of ancient Greek theater, a sort of contemporary mystery play. And in Europe, perhaps the greatest outlier within the postwar modernist avant-garde was Mauricio Kagel, who deconstructed the assumptions of concert protocol to create pieces that included movement, text, and instruments in ways counter to their "normal" purpose. But even here, we aren't quite to the tipping point, where we're speaking of more than just a particular niche of music. Instead, that tipping point toward a new art form emerges in the 1960s and really takes off by the 1980s, when "performance art" arrives. This has had its ups and downs over subsequent decades, but it clearly meets a need. More and more visual artists see it as at least a useful adjunct to their work, and some have made their entire careers out of a synthesis that cannot be categorized in any other way. (In a way, its refusal to accept traditional aesthetic taxonomy is analogous to the breaking of conceptual barriers that has allowed sound art and "music" to interpenetrate.) Laurie Anderson was perhaps the first performance artist to gain wide public recognition, emerging in the 1980s in tandem with the alternative punk, glam, and art rock scene of New York. Because she could play the violin competently, and had a wildly imaginative take on technologies warped toward her dramatic goals, she created a new form of urban storytelling, which merged song, spectacle, and cultural commentary. It remains a defining record of a critical moment when the gallery, club, and concert hall began to blur into a fluid venue.[12]

Anderson is an example of someone whose background is in the visual and fine arts, but who has created a substantial musical element in her work, and has to be considered with those more formally defined as "composers." But brilliant as she is, I still don't feel she is the most compelling example of this new synthetic practice. That role is taken up by Meredith Monk. One of the great pleasures of living long enough is to see certain artists *endure*, to watch their art grow as they continue to take chances and push their envelopes. Monk also comes from a different tradition of origin: she trained as a dancer as well as a singer. But from the outset the voice was always fundamental to her work, and in the fertile environment of New York in the 1960s, with cross-disciplinary movements such as Fluxus and the Judson Dance Theater, her approach found a welcoming home, a sort of "safe house" to explore a new world. Starting as a radical innovator, over the years it has become clear that her art is very much about achieving a sort of classical balance between its varied elements. In a Monk work, singing, movement, text (though often blurred or minimal), and instrumental sound combine in an exquisite harmony. More than any artist I know, her work suggests a kind of authentic folk practice, but from no single identifiable culture.

Monk by now is accepted as a composer, though it's taken a while for this to sink in on all but the most recalcitrant. Her materials are deliberately simple, but she has the good taste and intelligence to only write at the most *necessary* level, getting to essences (which doesn't mean it can't be difficult—just try to figure out the complexities of the "hocket-song" from *Facing North* [1992]). The template comes from American minimalism: the lines and harmonies are modal, and the form is cyclic patterning. It could be dull, but Monk's talent includes a killer app: she's congenitally unable to write an unhummable tune. As a result, I find the music always has an elemental quality, and it glows with an aura of authenticity. Her performances demand extraordinary precision of execution in a variety of modalities from her ensemble; in a sense it defines a new sort of multidisciplinary group virtuosity.

And while a sort of evening-long chamber theater piece is her default mode, her works list includes opera (*Atlas* [1991], commissioned by the Houston Grand Opera) and film (*Ellis Island* [1981] and *Book of Days* [1990][13]). The films in particular are haunting and original, and frankly it's a tragedy that she has not been allowed to make more, due to lack of funding. Monk has one other quality that distinguishes her from many other artists, and which is particularly clear in the films: she has enormous compassion for humans. Though her vision is clear and objective, it never abandons empathy. It searches for deep and real emotional understanding of what life throws at us. And I think that this vision is so broad that it demands Monk's multifaceted approach, her blending of so many media. It's not a trick or "kitchen-sink" approach; rather, it's *essential*.[14]

Before we conclude this exploration of the enlarged creative field in which we now find ourselves, we have to return to a concept and practice that has been touched upon in multiple ways throughout the chapter, but which demands a final accounting: *improvisation*.

The elephant in the room throughout has been jazz. Once again, it needs no justification as an art form; indeed, "classical" practice may be more needful of its influence and assistance now, a telling (and some would say just) reversal. But what I'm sensing is that the core element of jazz—improvisation—is becoming accepted trans-stylistically as a basic component of all American music. For its century-plus life, jazz has developed a sophisticated use of the technique that contains rules to distinguish correct from incorrect, and a series of adaptations of those roles from era to era so that the sound can evolve and ultimately find a new balance after a period of revolutionary turbulence. (For example, Louis Armstrong claimed that bebop was to his ear "Chinese music,"[15] yet it eventually became the most "classical" form of the art. And it was helped to this by George Russell, who played the role of Rameau through his harmonic theory of altered modes.[16])

Jazz has always had its great composers, who were able to direct brilliant creative players toward the goal of a personal vision (think Ellington, Mingus, Monk). They're in the pantheon now. The great bebop masters tended to advance a style and practice that was almost a "meta-composition": standards taken and reshaped into a new sound and way of playing (think Parker and Gillespie; from this font a series of more diverse individual voices poured: Davis, Coltrane, Mingus, Monk.) Post-bop, in the 1960s Free Jazz created an experimental avant-garde that pushed boundaries similar to the great revolutions in classical music at the start of the twentieth century (think John Coltrane, Ornette Coleman, Cecil Taylor). But in the 1970s both the importance of notated music in the mix and the influences from the classical avant-garde began to create a blend that was evermore difficult to categorize easily. The Association for the Advancement of Creative Musicians (AACM) began at this time in Chicago and from it emerged artists who saw the tradition as a source of freedom to explore realms that stylistically might never have been considered as "jazz" by their forefathers. Such composers as Anthony Braxton, Muhal Richard Abrams, Roscoe Mitchell, Henry Threadgill, George Lewis, and Leo Smith wrote music that demanded the same degree of attention to its abstract structures as any complex concert music, and chose freely whether to swing or not. Keith Jarrett developed a practice of spontaneous piano performance that felt comfortable within the traditional solo recital context. And a generation—Jason Moran, Uri Caine, Steve Coleman, Fred Hersch, Maria Schneider—now reaching its artistic maturity has made this blend of notation and improvisation, American and European models, yet again more fluid.[17]

The upshot is that if a composer feels that improvisation is in her blood, if it meets an expressive need, and if it comes from the roots of a familiar tradition, there is no longer any reason to exclude it from the most abstract, complex, or adventurous music. Indeed for younger composers of all backgrounds the question is becoming increasingly irrelevant, even puzzling to them to ask. And I find this to be an index of increasing health for survivable music.

There's one composer currently at his full powers who exemplifies this approach, and has achieved general visibility and acceptance beyond anything that seemed possible at the beginning of his career—John Zorn. He is a protean figure—composer, performer, promoter, and record producer. His music seems to have penetrated every possible venue: club, jazz festival, university, museum, opera house. He has created an enormous wash of music; indeed, it's not yet clear whether it's those pieces, or the nature of his career, that will be his true legacy. Beginning in downtown New York's structured improvisation scene in the 1980s, his reputation was established by a series of "game pieces," most famously *Cobra* (1984).[18] Creating a performance context where players could present a dizzying range of styles and languages under a single umbrella, united above all by split-second coordination of spontaneous events, he presented a vision where performers from different traditions could meet and exchange ideas and that very exchange became the point. And Zorn is an indefatigable performer (on both reeds and keyboards); he *has* "walked the talk" at every stage of his career.

All of these approaches to expanding the creative field are now available to younger composers, and they are sampling from them, each in his own manner. It's too early to see the most advanced and mature results, but I have to feel that this is one of the most significant shifts in the whole idea of composition we're seeing in this century. If the composer has been invested above all in creating a piece that is immutable object, then this shift will be scary. But I think even scarier will be the consequences if the new possibilities of the new openness are ignored.

All Together Now

At this point, having discerned many of the forces that will shape the composer's immediate future, we can begin to tie them together into a series of observations and recommendations. But before that, this chapter deals with one last piece of unfinished business. It's a postscript to what just preceded, and it enlarges the circle of openness one step further. Moving from the many forms of new choice and variety offered to the individual composer, this chapter suggests the opportunities and challenges that interaction with other composers and artists present. In short, it addresses *collaboration*.

The term has been trendy for some time now, and is in fact a buzzword of arts and academic administration, something that suggests another tiresome term "synergy." Let's try to forget that boilerplate for a moment and get back to essences.

Interaction of music with other disciplines is traditionally long and noble—ballet, incidental music for theater, film soundtracks, and of course opera have been ways to reach a far broader audiences than the concert stage alone. Let's accept that they continue to be an important part of any composer's output, and any chance to participate in them is welcome and should be seized. In this venerable tradition, perhaps there is no greater example than Philip Glass, who has not only created a body of opera that has redefined the medium but also emerged as one of the most original and effective film composers of the era.

And then there are artists pushing the envelope still further. For example, the recent "immersive theater" movement seems to have shaped a piece that has created a great deal of buzz, Chris Cerrone's *Invisible Cities* (2014), where the piece unfolds in a train station, the performers are mixed with audience (and often disguised so that their emergence as singers can be shock), and the distribution of the music throughout makes it impossible to hear as a whole (though audience members can get a more global feel for the score by wandering through the space with headsets tied to a central feed. The parallels to installation and sound art such as Cardiff's walks should be clear).[1]

But I'd like to think a bit about even more novel forms of collaboration that are emerging, ones that enlarge the very term. One of the simplest is the *composer collective*. While there have been groups of composers who established a profile based on a shared aesthetic (*Les Six* in France, the "Mighty Five" in nineteenth-century Russia), composers who band together administratively as well to present concerts of their own (and affiliated) works become more evident in the later twentieth century. *L'Itinéraire* is one example, Bang on a Can another, Boston's Composers in Red Sneakers an 1980s avatar, and Brooklyn's Sleeping Giant the current gold standard. This is a way of circumventing power structures that might otherwise keep younger composers outside the limelight. In fact, cultivating an aura of independence, it may make such composers more visible than otherwise possible, maybe even give a certain notoriety as a "salon des refusés." It also is useful for pooling resources when the cost of mounting concerts, publicity, and media distribution can be prohibitive for any lone artist, especially early in her career.

Another increasing phenomenon is projects with a defining theme and set of constraints, taken up by a group of participating composers. The new works can be in homage to a particular composer, piece, or historical anniversary; they can deal with a social or political issue; they can explore a particular instrumentation, often novel and looking for new repertoire; they can deal with the limitation of an extremely short duration. (More and more of us have participated in the "60 one-minute pieces by 60 composers" type of format.) I can't help but feel that part of the force driving this is that *there are just so many more composers now*. This comes from the overall global population increase, and it also is a reflection of the increased opportunities for training provided by formal education. There are more and more degree-granting composition programs, all the way through doctoral level. Alas, the last is starting to look like the story of the golden goose; initially such programs created a pool of academically qualified composers to fill the rising tide of new positions created in the United States after the Second World War. But the numbers of graduating students has continued to grow, and to ultimately outpace demand, leaving younger graduating composers now facing a far bleaker employment landscape. In light of this, it makes all the more sense for composers to try to take matters into their own hands, and in the new world of digital promotion, presentation, and social media, to forge a more independent route.

The next step in the widening circle is to bring the audience itself into the creative process. This phenomenon is very much in its infancy, and while I've witnessed several manifestations, I don't feel that it has yet found the right recipe to balance the input from a single creator with that from a larger group.[2] But the means are now with us. Instantaneous communication, combined with social media networks, seems poised to empower works where audience preferences, choices, and even direct submission of new materials all can be blended into a new whole. In this sense the composer may start to be more of a real-time DJ, sampling and mixing from an incoming information stream. A new way of thinking about branching decision-tree structure may be required to make this seem fresh and viable (it may help to have an open-form work that is first "composed" before it enters this realm; I witnessed a few years back a performance of *In C* devised by Ko Umezaki, who had designed a cell phone app so users could network to perform the work).[3] Though I'm getting out of my depth, it seems that video gaming may present a natural model for a new generation to explore this type of openness, both in devising an initial structure and then in finding ways to route and direct multiuser inputs so that a final result is always new, yet at the same time preserves some recognizable and recurrent global character. And even a greater challenge will be to find a way to make this amalgam resonate with the sense of "the whole greater than the sum of the parts," a quality we have always appreciated in enduring art.[4]

Because communications now exist on a simultaneous and truly universal scale, the other influence on collaboration we must all confront is *globalism*. Artists of every age, nationality, and culture can be in touch . . . if they can transcend the inherent niche-making tendencies of internet culture. Ever since the 1960s, world music has become a given in every composer's worldview. Not only are we exposed to music of worldwide range—"classical," traditional (folk), popular—but the opportunities have also multiplied to write for instruments previously excluded from or unknown to Western practice. (To take a personal example, I recently wrote a new piece for Chinese *zheng*; I also play *shakuhachi* modestly but seriously, as well as compose for it.) Yo-Yo Ma's Silk Road Ensemble is an extremely visible and somewhat commercial enterprise, but it has already commissioned a set of serious and questing composers to write for its mix of Western with Central and East Asian instruments. The Dutch composer Joel Bons won the 2019 Grawemeyer Award for *Nomaden*, a concerto for cello with an accompanying ensemble of similarly diverse instruments. Osvaldo Goljov has achieved genuine fame in his mix of Latin American with Eastern European Jewish practice, in particular the distinctive performance style of the Schola Cantorum de Venezuela in his *Pasíon Segun San Marcos* (2000).[5] It's far more likely now that a composer may end up writing a piece for a mix such as saxophone, *pipa*, and *dumbeck*. One can study the traditions of these instruments assiduously, but it will be difficult to integrate each with the other and preserve anything resembling traditional stylistic integrity. One approach may be to write for these instruments with a view to use their distinctive timbres and idiomatic performance gestures, but with no attempt at "authenticity." Mauricio Kagel took this route several decades back with his *Music for Renaissance Instruments* (1966).[6] The inverse is to appropriate the sounds and practices of non-Western music and apply them to traditional Western instruments. This is the impulse behind the music of George Crumb, albeit in a general and highly poetic manner. More ironic and deadpan, it drives the wit and energy of Steve Mackey's *Indigenous Instruments* (1989).[7] Or yet another approach is to create structures where each player can continue to perform within the tradition of his instrument, but the ensemble exists in a broader multi-stylistic framework, where other types of events and relations direct listening attention. Zorn's music naturally accepts this diversity, since it is more about the interaction of players than the actual content of their music, which stands as a kind of autonomous unit to be moved, like a piece in the "game." In some senses, he is writing for performers more than their instruments. It's also a reshaping of the Cageian practice of a "musiccircus," where a series of autonomous works are arranged and overlapped according to a master map, but one determined by chance operations.

And another byproduct of this interaction is greater *competition*. In particular, "classical" music has caught a new breath of life in East Asia, and some of the most successful composers nowadays are Chinese, starting with the first "invasion" of post-Cultural Revolution composers to Columbia and studies with Chou Wen-Chung: Chen Yi, Zhou Long, Bright Sheng, Tan Dun, Ge-Gan Ru, to name a few, followed by ever-increasing numbers since. Young American composers are no longer secure that they can promote their work within an insular community of fellow citizens. The world is hungry for the musical perspectives of other cultures, and the United States, despite its continuing ambivalence about immigration, in fact is one of the most open cultures of all for artists from outside its borders. This competition, on the one hand, may shut out deserving composers who need nurturance during the formative years of their careers: that's the downside. The upside is that they cannot ignore the challenge of other aesthetics and artists, no matter what their origin.

Truly this is a brave new world. Composers can collaborate with their colleagues and performers from anywhere on the planet, in a spirit of greater acceptance and exploration than ever. Performance resources exist across an instrumental spectrum unknown to previous generations. Real-time connections make simultaneous remote location performance finally feasible.

All of this is thrilling, and its growth in the field is unstoppable. There are just too many exciting and enticing facets to such collaborations for them to be resisted. And so, while accepting the inevitable, I want to pose a challenge, one that posits a risk that I think any composer must confront and surmount if she is to be successful and survive.

In the midst of this ferment, the sense of being part of a *community*, the composer may want to think twice. It's hard not to sound vaguely post-Marxian here, but the challenge I see is that of the *individual within the collective*. The problem is not how does one composer find a voice *and* recognition: the odds are already so stacked against either that it may only lead to madness to contemplate conquering both. Better to just work, appreciate the fact that one is even allowed to do so, and let the chips fall where they may.

Rather, the more pressing question now is how does one even *create* in an individual manner anymore? Between the necessity for increasing specialization in every domain, and the exactly inverse counterpressure to create comprehensive "multi-everything" art, how can any composer make work that he feels is worthy *and* that reflects his personal vision? What strategy can preserve the sense of a personal body of work? Are such questions even valid or relevant anymore?

In the art world, there is already an answer, provided first by Warhol and now by Jeff Koons—one conjures a concept and then creates a workshop of fabricators to realize the idea. It's actually a Renaissance practice, updated. In music, the great workshops of the most successful Hollywood composers have already perfected this practice to a state ideally suited to the commercial needs of their clients (the same can be said increasingly for all large-scale commercial pop, with producers the real stars and performers more "frontpeople" for the enterprise). It's really impossible to argue with this, as the culture celebrates this as the pinnacle of composerly achievement. (Indeed I tell my students that any argument I make for personal vision and art for its own sake may be the worst advice they can possibly get.) Perhaps in an increasingly interlinked and collaborative environment, it will be the only way a globally successful composer can achieve the dual goal of career recognition and an identifiably personal product (again think of Glass).

It's true that there are many who in fact have deep aesthetic ideals, but who also really don't care for the trappings of recognition, whether worldly fame or rarefied recognition. Despite my remark earlier about specialization, one of the evident byproducts of increasing openness I've described is the erasure of categories between different artistic practices and media, and a resultant lessening of specialization. As composers become more general in their practice, as they blend their role with performance, philosophy, multimedia, and a host of factors, it may become increasingly hard to hold onto a distinctive creative profile when so much involved in the process is so fluid and slippery. In the face of such pressures, there is no dishonor if one doesn't choose to be a persecuted "maverick." We need every committed artist we can get in every possible form.[8]

But there is a side of me, one that isn't an entirely objective observer of "future history," that hopes this is not the only option. We have a great paradox, a lesson in this issue's ambiguities, in the form of Cage. Never has a composer more rigorously striven through his life to shed his taste and ego in his creative product. Yet despite this attempt at aesthetic self-annihilation, I still can hear a Cage piece from almost any period and *it sounds like Cage.* So one of the glories of this "composerly" tradition is that it has allowed for outliers to show the rest of the world something it couldn't imagine collectively and yet *something it desperately needed*—think Bach, think Beethoven, think Mahler, think Ives, think Mingus, think Nancarrow, think (Meredith *and* Theolonius) Monk. The role of the composer is not only that of a musician who has mastered the focus group but who leads the audience by the sheer passion and authority of his vision. I think this still matters. In response to globalizing pressure, composers will either submit and conform to make a product they know their audience and fellow collaborators will love . . . or they will resist and *subvert*, creating music *of the time* in ways that listeners recognize, but that refuses to pander. It will accept the rules of engagement, but it will turn them on themselves, like classic martial arts, to both seduce the listener and undermine her assumptions. The relationship between the composer and her collaborators will be, by definition, different, but I hope they will preserve at the least one possible starting point—*with the composer.* This is the challenge, and I don't have any easy answer as how it's achieved. How do we play well in an increasingly collaborative environment, at all stages of the process of reception and creation, and still deliver music that refuses to merely divert us from the urgent task of understanding and sustaining our world?

Message in a Bottle

The time has come to start wrapping up. I've cast a wide net, but I want at least to attempt to make connections and draw conclusions from the topics I've broached. If I can't find an easy answer, perhaps I can pose questions that will be useful guideposts toward answers farther down the road. And here's the biggest question of all: "What then, *is* survivable music?" I'll now try at least to limn the outlines of an answer, even if I can't pin down every detail.

First of all, it seems clear to me that any potentially surviving music written today will have to deal with the issues I've raised:

The return of harmony
The rise of sonic essentialism
The minimalist conception of time flow, duration, and scale
The possibilities of technology
The practice of openness
The intersection between different media, art forms, aesthetics, and traditions
The pressure (both positive and negative) to collaborate with others, at increasing
     distances and of ever-greater difference

I don't believe that any composer has to develop a technique or approach dealing with every one of these issues into her practice. But I *do* feel strongly that we all have to confront what these issues represent. If we choose to reject any one, I think we need to know why. The very act of exclusion may become a great aesthetic strength, but only if it's done knowingly, not out of ignorance. In a sense, this is "meta" application of the old saying "you have to know the rules in order to break them." On the surface I think such a command is largely useless, an excuse to force conservative norms on questing spirits. But at a deeper level I agree. The historian and critic in me agrees with the composer. If one understands the most basic laws motivating successful art, then one can accept their spirit and develop one's own technical armature to achieve a vision that is more open and embracing. In this way we may even touch something "universal." And isn't *that* the very definition of what "tradition" is supposed to be about?[1]

So a composer needs to accept the fact that the twenty-first century is going to be dramatically different from its predecessor. I think most composers under the age of forty already know this intuitively. For them, the battles between tonality and atonality, serialism and minimalism, and modernism and romanticism are all moot points. In most cases they don't even *get* what the fuss was about. I think this is extremely healthy, because even though the aesthetic battles of the twentieth century were a matter of genuine passion and commitment on the part of their partisans, imbuing work with a particular strength, they also walled off too many from the beauties of their perceived "enemy's" music. More and more young people today are clearly not perceiving the sorts of social divides that have driven previous eras—and not just in aesthetics! They are breathtakingly open in matters of sexual preference and identity, race, ethnicity, and culture. Of course the promised land has not arrived—it is always possible to find strong pockets of intolerance in strongholds from Syria to Alabama (and even in supposedly "enlightened" locales such as my own state, Connecticut). But the demographic-attitudinal trend is clear, and I see it similarly reflected in the way younger composers now think of style, language, and technique.

At its worst, this can be an easy-going, "whatever" tolerance that forgives any technical flaw in the name of the moment's whim. But at its best it is a *refusal to refuse*, that is, not rejecting anything out of hand before its potential can be fully explored. And this tolerance is not only growing broader, I think it is also going deeper. In my generation, which came of age aesthetically in the 1970s, the Holy Grail was to find a way to reconcile tonality with atonality. One obvious manner was to juxtapose or even superimpose music of different harmonic practices. It opened up new vistas, but it could easily degenerate either into a sort of game of historical reference or only create facile contrasting effects. But at that very moment, most of my peers and I didn't know that a more comprehensive theory was emerging that actually proposed how to do that: spectralism. Like all theories, it had the potential to create works that met the system's demands, but remained fundamentally arid without the aid of a great artistic spirit. (And while many pieces from that first spectral wave certainly fall short, I still feel Grisey rises to a standard of greatness. And *that* is a proof of the individual creator's continuing power.) But as we move into the present, there's evidence that the movement has empowered a new form of sensual beauty and expressive power; one has only to look at the new Finnish school, in particular the music of Kaija Saariaho and Esa-Pekka Salonen.[2] And with the inclusion of more and more sounds from outside the pitched spectrum into the matrix of choice, the field grows broader and the possible theoretical constructs and connections evermore intricate and dazzling. So this process of synthesis is not just haphazard, contextual, or impressionistic. It has opened up new realms of rigor, though it may be successfully disguised beneath a beautiful surface . . . like Debussy.

The nature of my project here is partly revealed by the composers I've chosen to celebrate: Cage, Cowell, Partch, Messiaen, Mingus, Rochberg, Johnston, Ives, Riley, Reich, Xenakis, Feldman, (John C.) Adams, (Meredith) Monk, Grisey, (John L.) Adams, Zorn—to name but a few who have made an appearance. If one looks more closely at this list, these composers at first seem completely different from one another. And yet I also *know* they are all points on a continuous spectrum, rather than discrete entities hermetically sealed from one another. For one thing, they all are driven to explore *sound* in their music. That may seem so obvious as to be redundant; what composer doesn't deal with sound? But all too many in the last century became so enamored of the symbolic role of tones as to discount the primal impact of *sounds correctly arranged*. Based on this criteria, Cage and Xenakis might at first seem exceptions to my list, in that they were very much musical philosophers as well as composers. But the immediate visceral *impact* of their pieces remains an essential part of how we experience them.[3]

All of these composers also have combined wildly divergent influences into a personal blend. To take just two examples: (1) Feldman, for example, began his career within the experimentalist camp, yet almost despite himself, his immaculate ear and "visual" feel for beauty led him to create music of an increasingly romantic character, albeit like no romanticism previously known; and (2) no player could swing harder than Mingus, yet he pronounced a love for Beethoven, Bach, and Stravinsky (and you can hear it in both the gravitas and the wild jump-cuts of his music).[4]

Of course one can argue that every composer who develops a personal voice is synthesizing from a variety of influences. Point taken! But I would argue that ironically, because the *range* of such potential influences is wider than ever, composers who are able to find a guiding principle of synthesis between such increasingly divergent sources have the best chance to create the most survivable art. As time passes, we start to see the underlying connections between them more clearly. And this is what I'm getting at when I speak of an emerging common practice.

At the beginning of the twentieth century, before the greatest schisms had occurred, there are a series of composers who had already forged this sort of synthesis, who were effectively "postmodern" before there was even modernism. They are Ives, Mahler, and Debussy. (Similar but a little farther afield are Scriabin, Nielsen, Janacek, and Sibelius.) All three "opened the window" to the world about them and embraced what came through. In Ives and Mahler the mix of high and low, old and new, is obvious. Their embrace of the world is omnivorous ("Joycean" in its range: Mahler's status as a Jew within an increasingly intolerant Christian Central Europe opens a productive schism within his own music; Ives's transcendentalist outlook accepts the universe as a portal to spiritual enlightenment). Debussy is more rarefied and subtle, but the mix is still wide and seamless: Symbolist poetry; Impressionist and Japanese art; careful observation of nature; scientific calculation (albeit carefully disguised); Rosicrucian mysticism. Looking at them now from the vantage point of over a century, they seem far more similar than they ever could have appeared to their contemporaries. And they seem in this postmodern age (different, by the way, from "postmodern") to be more "contemporary" than ever.[5]

So we have two components from composer-models of the recent past: (1) a dogged attachment to the aural truth, the sonic immediacy of any piece they create, and (2) a crazily courageous willingness to blend divergent elements. Looking again at contemporary composers who have reached that point of maturity in art and career that benefits from retrospect, those that have united a variety of "streams" entering their creative consciousness, creating a broader "river" that exits as their work, seem to be making the biggest impact. Zorn mixes improvisatory practice with classical instrumentation and genres; John Luther Adams unites sound art, nature-centric transcendentalism, installation, process-driven algorithmic music, and American experimentalism; Osvaldo Golijov is blending popular and classical traditions from both Latin America and Europe; Kate Soper has blended performance art, pop music stylings, philosophy, history, and classic music-drama forms. I am not arguing that these are the greatest composers of their generation, but I *am* positing that they have stayed aware of the forces moving new music, and have been able to exert their own creative counterpressure on them to create a personal statement: no mean feat.

Finally, if I were to look for a model along these lines from composers who have either completed or almost finished the arc of their work, I would cite two:

First, a European, recently deceased: György Ligeti. To me he looks like the single greatest postwar composer within the Western classical tradition, yet his music is hardly homogeneous; it has a protean quality, shifting throughout his career through a string of passionate obsessions, driven by insatiable curiosity. It renewed the contact with the very feel and fabric of sound via its textural experiments of the 1960s. It opened up a wild, quasi-Dada theatrical practice in pieces like *Aventures* and *Nouvelles Aventures* (1962, 1965), which was to find a more traditional flowering in his opera *Le Grand Macabre* (1977, rev.1996). It stayed open to the most varied influences, ranging from pygmy music to American minimalism to the rhythmic experiments of Conlon Nancarrow. It rethought classical practice in a works such as the Horn Trio and the Preludes. And it moved into a fascinating hybrid of just intonation with equal temperament in such late works as the Violin and Horn Concertos (1993, 2002).[6]

For an American composer, still with us, I would cite Frederic Rzewski. So many of these strands come together in his oeuvre. One could criticize it as too limited, since it is primarily piano music, but then one can say the same of Chopin. He is a brilliant player, and has never lost touch with the visceral reality of performance. He has never been afraid of improvisation or technology; even now he is part of the pioneering live electronic improvisation group MEV (along with Alvin Curran and Richard Teitelbaum). The influence of folk and popular music of a wide range of cultures is omnipresent in his work. His music has always embraced a dizzying range of styles and languages, but it is simultaneously shaped by structures that are tied to modernist rigor. And yet his early works are now classics of minimalism, such as *Les Moutons de Panurge* (1968), *Attica* (1972), and *Coming Together* (1971). Indeed, he has that thing that perhaps every composer needs if he wants to survive—a single game-changing piece. In Rzewski's case it is *The People United Will Never Be Defeated* (1975), a set of variations on a Chilean leftist folk song that reaches audiences of all levels, is wildly inventive, and never avoids virtuosity for the sake of false anti-elitism.[7] And as is clear from this description, his work has always been motivated by a sincere and intense political component, one that rages against injustice.

And *that* suggests a third and final component, perhaps the most important one of all, in what I see will make music "survivable." It's going to sound strange at first, but I'll put it out and then elaborate. This music will have to be *more than just music.*

No, I'm *not* suggesting that all music must become programmatic or that a good social or political intention or reference is enough to excuse the lack of craft. Let me be clear: the act of creating a convincing, expressive, imaginative piece of music is a miracle. It should not need more justification than that. If one can make such an artifact, one can face death with a certain satisfaction. But history is not always sympathetic to good intentions, sincerity, or even technical brilliance. And this takes us back to the whole issue of a term I broached at the beginning, *absolute music.*

I wonder whether the great divide between the audiences and the composers of what has been called concert, classical, or art music really didn't occur because of chromaticism and atonality, but rather because music moved to a previously unknown level of abstraction and self-declared separation from the world at large. After all, the very idea of "absolute music" is a nineteenth-century concept, and thus is quite young (first coined by Wagner [of all people] in a review in 1845).[8] The idea that a piece of music can move one into a realm of abstraction, and a sort of spiritual awakening with no other means than its sound, is certainly seductive. But in the glory days when this *was* the case—the Middle Ages and Renaissance—music was the handmaiden of the church; the text of any mass or motet gave a justification to the sounds that allowed a huge range of expression, even the brilliantly arcane constructions of Ockeghem. In the common practice, Western classical music seemed to finally achieve this goal. But when one looks more closely at the repertoire, fewer and fewer pieces remain truly "absolute." Most of the Beethoven symphonies become grand metaphors for superhuman states—the Third heroism; the Sixth nature; the Seventh dance; the Ninth worldwide community. Even his late quartets begin to sound like a crazy-quilt of all human experience and emotion, perfectly formed yet also garbled in the way that life has of tripping itself up. Perhaps only Bach in a few pieces such as *Art of the Fugue* comes close to that purest state, where the simple, perfect correspondence of tones is sufficient . . . except for the fact that it then becomes a type of metaphor for the ideal God-clockwork-heaven in which he believed.

Until the second half of the twentieth century! What *is* Boulez's *Structures* about? The answer is simple: itself. It is brilliant, and I can testify similarly that anyone who takes the time to analyze the work of Milton Babbitt will discover that his pieces are some of the *cleverest* ever written, in creating comprehensively coordinated relationships between musical elements.[9] But they exist more in the aforementioned symbolic realm than the acoustic. (There's a word for this: solipsism.) And even if we are thinking of music as a metaphoric representation of scientific and technological issues, Xenakis seems a far more effective example, as one can much more clearly *hear* the intended phenomena and processes in play. Likewise, though often lumped into this camp, Elliott Carter in fact wrote music that consistently evoked the pace and interaction of everyday life, through his hyper-sophisticated rhythmic inventions; they created a flow that was at once genuinely vernacular and dramatic, despite the forbidding surface.

Again, I'm not saying that absolute music is wrong or bad. It *is* elitist, but all art needs elitism, in order to carve out possibilities, to shake up thinking. What is problematic is if such elitism becomes a norm, and if an art form loses touch with its roots. Frankly, the sort of experience that audiences in the nineteenth century had—a piece that moved their soul, that they heard in their dreams, that they carried with them through the day—is now the realm of popular music. A great song or album (no longer a physical artifact, but a downloadable package) will speak to people in an immediate way that I fear a great symphony no longer will (though I can always hope).

So does this music I've been talking about—art/concert/postclassical—have any future? The answer is *yes*, and it's one to carry us forward. I believe that it has unique virtues and special strengths that make it important, even essential to the art. It is a necessary complement to the global popular music (much of it fantastic) that currently rules the discourse. Without it, we will be impoverished, and will only know what we've lost when it's too late, like a beautiful species essential for our survival that suddenly goes extinct. (Think bees.)

Perhaps a better way to frame this is not to claim that music of a special substance must interact with other issues and disciplines . . . or die. Rather, it should be that music is seen as the ideal medium to represent a singular interplay of elements. It can remain itself, and yet the sounds can begin to take on roles and meanings that go beyond themselves, that serve to reshape our understanding of our world. It is this—the unique combination of the symbolic *and* the acoustic—that gives ambitious/serious/concert music such power. It can move us in the moment, and even after it has passed, we feel we have experienced a vision beyond our comprehension. It will take us into a new dimension that is its own justification, yet it leaves a residue that aids us as we carry it into our daily struggle to find meaning.

Yes, this sort of music I propose cultivates a certain abstraction. But precisely because of that, it has the possibility of becoming a "meta" field of play in which we can envision new relationships among the components of our lives, possible solutions to seemingly intractable problems.[10] *I feel that no other field of human endeavor has the capacity to unite so many strands of our emotional, intellectual, philosophical, scientific, cultural, natural life . . . and to create a viable, independent life-transforming object in the process.* I feel the circumstances that are now emerging, rather than marginalizing music, are in fact relentlessly pushing it back into a role it must play, to aid our culture as it strives to adapt to the almost inhuman pressures threatening to crush it.

So composers, the field is wide open. The challenge is clear: we all need not just to write survivable music, we need to exploit its inherent strengths to *make music survive.* And in the process *it will help us to survive.*

After that rousing peroration, a few final words to those joining the dance. May they not seem too much like a commencement speech. They are addressed to the younger composers I cited at the very beginning.

You have it tough practically. Academic jobs have dried up, and sinecures of the past are vanishing. The "contemporary college *kappelmeister*" will soon be a thing of the past. This role defined the idea of a concert composer for a generation, but it was suited to a very particular time and place, and perhaps an aberration in the composer's true societal role. Fortunately, there were alternative models percolating: the rock savant personified by Zappa; the minimalist band leader, represented by Reich, Glass, and now Paul Dresher; the composer-conductor, as embodied by John Adams; the Svengali producer in the form of Brian Eno; and the itinerant performer-composer, in the form of Kurt Rhode, Lisa Bielawa, and Derek Bermel. I suspect these are going to be among the viable models for the immediate future (and not the only ones). Add to them composers who write for multimedia, especially independent film, video, and games. Life is going to be more like the way it's always been for most composers: hardscrabble, day-to-day, hand-to-mouth.

For this, coming from one in the boomer generation, you have my apology. Life should have been better for you, and instead many horizons are contracting. To be frank, it sucks. I don't think enough people recognize the burden of survival that is being forced upon you, or are willing to make any reasonable sacrifice to aid your finding a place in the societal structure.

In addition, there is now a burgeoning awareness of how restrictive and closed our world of "art music" has been. The centuries-long exclusion or denigration of women and people of color is a shame that must be acknowledged. If the field is to grow and thrive, this exclusivity must be turned to *inclusivity.* It may make it easier for those previously on the outside, but harder for those who assumed a smoother road was unchallengedly theirs. There will be resentments, schisms, and heartbreak along the way. But I can also say that the wave of exceptional "marginal" music now cresting—from women, LGBTQ, and people of color—is justification for following this course, for nurturing new energies and visions.

And then there is a *big* issue that this chapter can only glancingly touch, but that you will have to face. We are approaching a turning point in our relation as a species to the earth as our home. It's entirely possible that all the issues I've raised will be washed away by an environmental shift of supra-historical dimensions. I'm speaking about climate change. It is possible that everything I've written about technologies and styles may seem hopelessly trivial in comparison to the shift that will occur in your lifetime. You may actually be fated for—at best—what Bill McKibben calls "the soft landing."[11] This is such a big topic that if I pursued it further it would be the subject of another essay at least as long, probably a separate book. In short form, the state of our environment is going to be a topic you cannot ignore. Remember how I said above that music needs to be about more than music? This well may be the mother of all subjects you will have to interpret and confront. I suspect you are going to have to find ways to connect with nature that go way beyond things like spectralism and "sonic essentialism." And you may have to collaborate in ways that aren't just aesthetic, but that may involve literal survival.

It's possible, some would say probable, that the odds favor the cataclysmic. But we have to do all we can to try to mitigate the potentially horrible, then do the best with the hand we've all been dealt, in this moment. Accept that there is serious danger ahead, prepare yourself for it. But also try to deal with the factors discussed here, treat them seriously, acknowledging the threat on the horizon, but keep moving forward with what you know you can do.

Ultimately, there are two things that give me hope and that I suspect you already know them without my saying. One is that the flip side of the lousy hand you've been dealt is freedom. The emerging digi-social networks (so long as the electricity holds) give you a chance to create your own market and maybe even bypass gatekeepers and those very societal structures that might strive to shut you down or out. You may be able to crowd-source your way to a real sustaining audience: not huge, but enough to make ends meet. Remember, it doesn't matter how many people listen, only *enough* to support you, and the *right sets of ears.*[12] This might ultimately be your tribe around the campfire. Screw the rest.

The other hopeful thing is what I've been trying to expound in this chapter. There is a convergence of emerging factors that is going to make survivable music necessary, maybe even cool again. All you have to do is ride the wave.

I end with not my own words but that of a young composer who sent me this statement a while back. For me it touches many of the bases that I've tried to broach here. It bespeaks of clarity and idealism in wonderful balance. I'll step aside and let the next wave speak:

> I attempt to continue the work of composers like Varèse, and so many others thereafter, who dreamt of the infinite possibilities of development for any timbre; who were obsessed by the sounds of man-made objects, and hoped that one day, we would gain control over such objects to create a beautiful sonic environment that could only be matched by nature itself.
>
> In a world where everything is connected, everyone is looking for some sort of deeper meaning, and interactiveness is of growing importance, I aim to create sound, and invite others to create sound, in an attempt to connect humans with one another, and create deeper connections with the natural world, despite the stigma that technology often does just the opposite.[13]

Re Me

Like any artist, I can readily talk at length about myself, but in the preceding text I felt I needed to keep my creative persona somewhat in the background, as I was striving hard to take as broad and open a view as I could. But if readers have stuck with me this long, then this may be the point that I can step forward. This chapter is thus in two parts: first, personal history and then a closer look at the musical practice I've developed, especially over the past roughly twenty years. The first part is *not* a memoir, even though it spotlights a series of events and decisions from my life. *That* can wait for another time, if needed. But I do think it's useful to set the stage for how the practice I now call my own developed, the strands that wove together to produce something that now feels quite whole to me. And by reading this, I think it will retrospectively cast light on many of the observations and opinions in the preceding chapters.

1 A Life Saved by Music

When one reaches a certain age, some things just get murkier and more difficult, but happily others start to fall into place . . . or at least into perspective. In the latter category falls an inkling of some direction and shape to the arc of one's life. Things that earlier, when I was immersed and enmeshed in them, seemed confusing and impenetrable suddenly appear a lot more obvious. Choices made link suddenly with other choices in a way that suggest a larger matrix, a more focused motivation, if not a plan. So it is when I look back on how I found music and it found me.

It didn't seem predestined. The United States doesn't have the sort of coordinated early arts education of many other cultures, and in my case, though I received a fine education in elementary and high school, the arts and serious music were largely nonexistent. I took piano lessons as a child but quit near fifth grade because I wasn't allowed to learn pop songs. In retrospect I see that wasn't exactly the reason—I think I wanted some sort of contemporary music as part of my diet, and it was the only point of reference I had. I also now remember that while I seemed to have some facility at the keyboard, I don't remember actually *hearing* what I was playing. I was more of a trained animal, performing a trick.

So I quit, and basically guaranteed that I would not be a performer when I re-engaged with music later. In my high school freshman year I had a remarkable French teacher who, after he'd performed some miracles with us (like having us read Gide's *Symphonie Pastorale* and discuss it in French), decided in the last two weeks of classes to give us a pocket sketch of the history of Western music culled from his record collection. He, a proto-hippie, was cool in our eyes, so this classical music didn't seem so alien in his hands as a sort of Pied Piper/DJ. I was the one who bit, and began to listen on my own, collecting LPs. I should have known something was up when the first two discs I bought were the Bach Brandenburgs and the Carter string quartets (see, things *do* become clearer with distance).

I began to take piano lessons again near the end of high school and felt an increasing need to write things down. A few tentative efforts weren't very satisfying, and I went to college expecting to be a history major, maybe pre-law, and to explore music as a sweet avocation.

I went to Yale, which has a great musical tradition, and again retrospect shows that my choice was musical, that is, largely driven by the great concerts I heard during my college trip in fall 1971. I was a history major from beginning to end, and to this day don't regret it. Because I had so many Advanced Placement credits, I entered school with no distributional requirements, so I was able to take as many music courses as I wanted, and missed being a double-major or music minor because, ironically, I didn't take the music history sequence. There were just too many other fascinating history courses. But almost until the end I really didn't believe I could ever be part of the world of music; everyone I saw in it was so far ahead of me, had so much experience already.

But two people reached out and gave me gifts that allowed me to change my course. The first was the composer and theorist Jonathan Kramer, who allowed me into the sophomore composition class and simply took me seriously. (Some of the best advice I ever received was when he countered my self-doubts with, "The moment you put a note on paper you became a composer, so stop worrying whether you can call yourself one. Worry about being a good one.") In retrospect his interests (above all, in time and postmodernism) were almost ideal for my own, but I didn't know that, as mine were in such an embryonic state. He just pressed me to write. And the act of taking a piece all the way through to fruition was the most important test I could pass at that moment. For the final class concert I wrote a song cycle for baritone and six instruments based on anti-war poems of Siegfried Sassoon, and when my singer dropped out I sang and conducted the whole thing . . . and lived to tell the tale.

The other person who came to my rescue was Charles Ives. The year 1974 was his centennial and overlapped my sophomore and junior years. In an outpouring of collegiate zeal celebrating an alum, and combined with the countercultural vibe of the early 1970s, Yale went all out, and I heard a huge range of his music live (including John Kirkpatrick playing the Concord Sonata). With some composers, I think I would have been overwhelmed and intimidated by the craft and polish, but somehow Ives seemed to be giving permission with every note. The mandate was above all to follow mind, spirit, imagination. The music made perfect sense to me, and still does (only now I'm more awed by it than ever). And by my senior year, I wrote a tone poem clearly influenced by the opening of Ives's Fourth Symphony, which I submitted to the undergraduate orchestra composition competition, and to my astonishment, won. As soon as I heard my piece played by the Yale Symphony, I was gone, hook-line-sinker (and on the program were also Ives, Ruggles, Barber, and Copland; my fate was sealed as I heard my ancestors surrounding me, bucking me up). It also helped to convince my parents that I'd not gone mad, throwing away what had seemed a predestined scholarly career. From that moment on they were always the best supporters, even if they found my work puzzling (a situation I've heard countless times from fellow composers).

So one of the things that shaped me profoundly was a late start. I feel I've been catching up ever since. And having made a sudden hard right (or left) turn in my life, I then made a series of choices that shaped me for the rest of my life. I pretty much knew what I was getting into, but perhaps the thing I couldn't see as clearly was how deeply grounded these choices were in basic assumptions and beliefs, even if unconscious. And here are a few of them:

In my education I chose outsiders as teachers. Jonathan Kramer was a brilliant intellectual maverick, and to this day is better known as a thinker than a composer, though his music is extremely original (one of the most unusual blends of minimalist with modernist practices I've ever heard, followed by a suite of pieces which took "postmodernism" seriously as a fully integrated and realized technique and aesthetic). In fact, his thinking on time in music, and its various manifestations, would be critical to my own developing ideas and practice. My working with him was serendipity; I had no idea who he was when I knocked on his office door my sophomore year. But afterward I did find three teachers who each gave me either a great conceptual or a technical gift: George Rochberg, Ralph Shapey, and Iannis Xenakis.

Certainly these were all celebrated figures in the field, and my labeling "outsiders" might seem strange. Unlike my friend John Luther Adams, who studied with Lou Harrison and James Tenney, two composers with impeccable "maverick" credentials, my three might seem much more establishmentarian. But all three lived in an uneasy and often confrontational relation with said establishment: it couldn't ignore them, but also found them off-putting. Rochberg of course foreswore and denounced postserial modernism as far too insular and expressively limiting. Shapey so despised the whole scene that he placed a moratorium on performance of his work for almost a decade. And Xenakis, though endlessly feted throughout his career, was not at the center of Parisian musical life when I lived there—his class at the Sorbonne was small and open to all, while the "real" action was under Boulez's eye at IRCAM.

In the end, I searched out each of these composers because I felt they had something I needed, and I admired the music. And I wasn't disappointed. At the start, I had no idea that Kramer's obsession was with different ideas and manifestations of time in music, something that would drive my own music ever afterward. Rochberg's simultaneous embrace of the past and the present in his breakthrough works (from his String Quartet No. 3 on) excited the side of me that was a historian, and also opened a playing field that was Ivesian in its amplitude and diversity. He also was the only composer from whom I ever felt I received a "moral education" . . . even if I disagreed with much he espoused.

Shapey wrote in a hyperpassionate modernistic vein that blended elements of Schoenberg and Varèse. The American accent added to this reminded me of Carl Ruggles, a composer whom I embraced early in my listening and study (I wrote my dissertation essay on *Sun-Treader*). But above all he was the only teacher who really taught me nuts-and-bolts *technique*. From him I learned how to write a phrase, and then how to combine different phrase structures and lengths to create genuine counterpoint.

And Xenakis (with whom—full disclosure—I did not study privately, but took a class on his techniques that he taught for one year, along with about five other people) finally settled questions of form for me. What before had always seemed either narrative, theatrical in nature or a series of traditionally bequeathed molds (AABA, etc.) suddenly became an object in space, let loose in time, and the celestial geometry of it thrilled me, providing the key to a first wave of works I felt was created under a common concept.

But as I look back now, and with greater perspective, I see that all these composers were, despite their success, controversial. They tended not to be "polished" in the way of many composers, whose "professional" credentials are impeccable. Even Rochberg, whose traditionalist (read common practice tonal) technique was often daunting, could create moments of disturbing self-exposure or juxtapositions that pushed the boundaries of accepted taste. In short, I realize now that I chose mentors who were not the suavest politicians. But then, what was I thinking if I had taken Charles Ives as my model to begin with?

I served a long apprenticeship, and long after I finished formal education. Because I started late, I didn't feel as though I was dragging out my education by attending graduate school. Everything was new, and I was in "catch up" mode. Thus I'm a composer who got a doctorate because I felt I needed the time to study, more than just a union card for a job (though that was also clearly a part of the deal). And I felt the need to study with particular individuals. The teachers I've mentioned I feel were exceptional for me; there were a few others I might have worked with had they and their programs accepted me, but since they didn't, I can only assume it was fate that I ended up with the crew I did.

And after school, I feel I went through a long period, about fifteen years, where my voice was slowly maturing and my vision clarifying. Part of it was just learning craft, confronting various challenges and problems in one piece after another, feeling I had passed a series of tests. Beyond that self-imposed education, the me that had planned to be a historian asserted itself in two ways. First, in the spirit of much music at the height of postmodern practice, I was quite free in blending languages from different styles and historical periods. Modernist atonality and chromatic tonality could exist cheek-by-jowl, though I felt that ultimately they needed to find a way to coexist in a larger (and more unified) space. Certain pieces had them emerge from one another, or one was "framed" by the other. My first piano sonata *Spiral Dances* (1984) was this sort of journey, and a curious sextet (piano trio plus violin/viola/harp) *Time/Memory/Shadow* (1988) took a little Elgaresque march I wrote in early in college and "excavated" it over the course of the piece until it appeared in its original form, something I dubbed "personal archeology."

Time was for me both symbolic, represented by different historical styles, and also more abstract (yet paradoxically more visceral), a space in which events could unfold with an amplitude of spirit. I wrote a series of pieces that had an omnibus title *Time Is a Sphere*, all based on a global view of form that was *literally* global, a legacy of my encounter with Xenakis. My first string quartet, *A Path Between Cloud and Light* (1985) suggested both an organic growth and a cyclic process of development, and in retrospect feels like a milestone along this road. But in the end my idea of space was not going to create music of the scale and depth I wanted until I allowed my thinking on harmony to move to a new level and enter into that very space, redefining it. But *that* is the topic of the second half of this chapter.

I've loved to travel. There's a side of me that is very much the tourist. I've headed off to Europe repeatedly, and Asia is now a greater part of my travel repertoire. I've been to more colonies and residencies around the world than you could shake the proverbial stick at. I've felt a deep need to engage with other cultures at various levels of depth (I speak fluent French and near-fluent Italian). I've always wanted to see cultural landmarks in the flesh. (Part of it is feeling what a place really is in situ. The geographical reality is almost always different from what you expect, no matter how prepared you are.) And that "tourism" applies in a more general way to my interests, especially in other art forms. Literature, visual arts, and film make life worth living for me. I constantly try to keep up with news of politics, science, and sociology. I can't claim to be a polymath, but my curiosity is at least polymathic.

Two times I have lived abroad in ways that were life-changing. The first was in 1980–81, when I went to Paris on fellowship. The encounter with Xenakis was the most important single fruit for my work of that trip, but there were countless other ways I was engaged and changed. I came to realize how different European and American aesthetics are (we are more naïve, but we also know a much broader range of art, in part due to the necessity of keeping an ear to the ground for popular trends). Over a single season I went to 100 new music concerts (an exact figure, though total coincidence) and gained an invaluable feel for the range and focus of European music. And living in France was particularly good for me, as it is really the most alien of all Western European cultures to an American. That may sound strange, but all the other nationalities have strong ethnic presences in the United States—the French presence is far more in the realm of culture and consumer luxury than day-to-day (unlike in Canada). And above all, I came to appreciate the critical importance of color/timbre as a structural tool in composition. Before, I had always seen orchestration as a means to "clothe the model," to put a final layer of sound on a Platonic structure. Now I realized a perfect surface could be an end in itself.[1]

And the other voyage was decades later, with a three-month residency in Japan (2007). I had always wanted to go to Japan, whose classical and contemporary music spoke to me in a primal way, so simultaneously exotic and yet comprehensible. In meeting and interviewing Japanese composers, touring throughout the country and visiting a host of temples and historic sites, drinking in the extraordinary energy and imagery of Tokyo, I felt the same thrilling shock of sheer *difference* as I had when I first landed at Charles de Gaulle. And I think my music came to a new visceral appreciation than ever before of the momentary, the ephemeral, and of silent but implicit energy.

But the very range of this curiosity is I think a double-edged sword. On the one hand, it's given me endless ideas for my work and made me feel that all my creative activity is a great game on the broadest possible playing field. On the other, though, perhaps I have been something of a gadabout, whizzing from one location to another both physically and intellectually, perhaps not settling into as deep and focused an engagement with music as I should. I can't dismiss that criticism, and I also think that's the way such range is often perceived in the field. But I also can't regret my interests, and if I may have paid some for them, I still think they've been essential. And in the past decade or so, I also feel the type of more focused engagement has finally emerged, just when it had to.

I've spent a life in academia. Most of the composers I knew and admired as I "grew up" as a composer were also teachers. I had always assumed I would be a teacher, even before I found music. So it was not hard for me to enter university teaching as a vocation, and have the institution as a patron. And I can say that where I ended up, very early in my career, and stayed, was good for my art. The Hartt School is a serious conservatory in the Northeast, with stimulating colleagues with whom I've spent the majority of my mature life, and individualistic, serious students. They come from all different perspectives on the field, and their openness to the issues that once divided all of us has been an inspiration to me, and in part an inspiration for this book (as well as a personal confirmation of its theses).

It has also been a wonderful laboratory for my work, resulting in performances and recordings of pieces by students and faculty in everything from solo to symphony. I've lived the life of the twentieth- and twenty-first-century *kappellmeister*, even with my far-flung travels. (Through the 1980s and 1990s, I also was a member of a Boston composer collective, Extension Works, which gave me a series of opportunities to write for ensembles of young professionals and gain an excellent archive of chamber works.)

But of course there is again a downside. One friend once told me that the danger of being a music professor is that you're surrounded by younger people who actually think you may know what you're doing. And it's true, you *are* in a situation where you often know more than anyone else, except your colleagues, and they're too "collegial" to challenge you.

But beyond that potential trap, I feel a shift in the way society views the composer-teacher. In the emerging generation, by far the most successful have established a creative profile first, and then parlayed it into a college position if they so desired. In some cases, there has been a backup of family/trust-fund wealth that has made that route possible (the hiatus before the fulltime job, a kind of "meta version" of the "gap year"), but I'm not carping. Virgil Thomson dissected all this nearly a century ago in *The State of Music*.[2] Composers are so far outside the mainstream that their understanding of how to work the sociology of the field is itself a sort of composition in its own right. So I salute those who are willing to use whatever they had in hand to advance their career arc, so long as they keep their eye on the music itself. Ultimately though, in the world's view, touching on a certain innate American anti-intellectualism, academics aren't cool, artists are. If you get labeled too much or too early as the former, you may have problems down the road.

But then I must turn around and cite one final asset to the gig. It's been close to New York, and after about ten years of centering my efforts on Boston, I turned my focus southward. In some ways it's been a case of "so near, yet so far" career-wise. But that distance, and the relative safety of my little school, has meant a certain freedom to pursue my own course, less buffeted by trends and fashions . . . even though I remain very much aware of them. I'm not sure I would have what feels like a certain clarity on many levels of creation and perception without this context. And it's entirely possible that if I'd moved to the City early, I would have been thrown to the dogs and eaten alive.

I write words. And lots of them. Because of my late start in music, and my humanities training, I have always been a capable writer of expository prose. It has helped in several ways; for one thing, early on, as I was desperately "catching up" in my musical training, my articulateness reassured folks that I either knew what I was doing or eventually would. As I discovered the world of critical writing, it plugged me into pre-internet information networks (i.e., free CDs) that kept me abreast of an enormous amount of music in the world that I would never be able to hear live otherwise. I wrote a book about *In C* that gave me the entrée to talk to a host of inspiring elders of American experimentalism. And that constant demand to give verbal form to my thoughts and intuitions always spilled into both my teaching and my "recycling" of thoughts into a constantly evolving practice. The full text you've just read is a sample of what's always going on in my mind. In a sense, along with the teaching, it is the one thing I do *other than* composition that might be called virtuosic (in the sense of fluent, precocious, without much seeming effort).

But of course there's a downside here as well, and it's perhaps the most serious one. There is always a certain skepticism within the musical community of those deemed too skilled verbally. There's a sense that, maybe following the "two hemispheres" brain-model, there's room in a single creative mind for notes or words, but not both. Virgil Thomson and Ned Rorem have always had to fight the fact that their literary voices were often valued more than their musical ones. Even for Ives, the fact that he wrote a sort of original, cranky, and voluble prose is seen by some as proof of his fundamental amateurism. *They* say, "You should say it in sounds alone; you must have a deficiency if you need to voice it in words as well."

And then there's the fact that unless you only write manifestos or treatises explaining your own work, you are in the service of others. Thomson pegged it when he said that writing about "other men's music" (let's now change that to "other people's music") places you in their service, and marks you as a servant, or at best, an accomplice. In any case, you move a rung down the ladder of estimation.

Yet I admit I've always admired composers who created texts parallel to their music. And the finest among them are Stravinsky and Schoenberg with *Poetics and Music* and *Style and Idea*; Cage with his great sui generis sequence starting with *Silence*; Debussy's, Schumann's, and Berlioz's remarkably personal journalistic criticism; Ives's *Essays Before a Sonata*; Louis Andriessen's imaginatively unfettered analysis of Stravinsky, *An Apollonian Clockwork*; and Bernstein's *The Unanswered Question*. Yes, we probably would not read these works if the composers who wrote them were ciphers. But because of their creative accomplishment, we want to enter their minds, and as words are a common medium for all of us, they help us better to understand these artists' creative stance when they speak to us.

So I like to think about music, which makes me talk and write about it. So be it.

Matters of the Spirit matter to me. I'm far from the only composer to sense a spiritual dimension to music, and indeed many are more overtly committed to the divine and mystical in their art than I. But I *do* feel that music is almost a parallel universe or dimension to the one we inhabit in the visceral world. It's abstract, yet as palpable, maybe more so, than any experience. It may well predate language.[3] The American transcendentalist ethic was one that appealed to me from the moment I encountered it. Music is a portal to something beyond; it actually inspires belief for me, even if I'm reluctant to define what I *believe in* (other than music itself). So I can't help but take it very seriously. Of course, I feel there is always room for a lightness of touch and the spirit of play. It's necessary in fact. Satie grows more wondrous with each encounter. Gershwin is a miracle. If one can reach their heights of invention and expression, it's a triumphant life.

But ultimately I'm drawn to music that attempts to create a world that's both as rich as this one, yet also suggests an ideal on another level. That's an illusion, I know, but it's also a goad to creativity and a goal through which to channel ambition toward less selfish things. It also can make you seem a little too serious in some eyes. But in the end I respond more to enlightenment than diversion.

And over the past couple of decades I have become Buddhist. Not in a specific sect or single practice, but in a serious way nevertheless (for the record, I've found a personal mix in Jodo Shin and Soto Zen). Almost every day now I read from sutras, play the shakuhachi, and meditate. One concept of the religion is that there is a universal Mind, the thing we come from and return to. I can't help but feel that music, in its universality, abstraction, and immediacy, may be the closest thing possible to that Mind. I don't try to celebrate Buddhism's philosophy in music, but I know that its precepts shape my practice and give me focus.

I can't ignore tradition. There's no doubt that my initial attraction to composition came from the American mavericks/ultramodernists. And they *are* an experimentalist bunch, pushing boundaries and smashing through standards of taste and polish. They do things that often seem "unmusical" to the guild. I've always loved that quality of freedom and fearlessness one receives in listening or performing their work.

And at the same time, I've never wanted to deny the classical tradition that's basically Eurocentric. Indeed, Ives himself is a prime example of this. Really, what else would one expect of a composer who can juxtapose quotations of Brahms and "Pigtown Fling" in a single piece?[4] His two "fathers" are clearly (1) his own biological/experimental, George, and (2) his pedagogical/traditional, Horatio Parker (and no matter how much Ives denigrated the latter, it's clear that he delivered a great deal of essential information and craft to the young composer).

So I can't ignore the wildness of Schumann, Debussy's scary innovation disguised under the loveliest surface, the perfect balance of horizontal and vertical in Josquin and Bach. Mahler remains a pinnacle for me, similar to Ives, in the capacity to contain a world-embracing range of voices and expressive states. But as I grow older, I also marvel more and more at Brahms, his ability to saturate a piece with so much information and it still remain crystal clear.

I don't believe that one should bow down submissively to their accomplishment. Though most of us are fated to fall short of the standard that "survivable music" sets up, it doesn't mean we shouldn't try. By now I think of my relationship as a *robust argument with tradition.* I want to find the deepest successful principles that animate and motivate this music, and drag them kicking and screaming into a fresh context. And if that's too aggressive a metaphor, then let's say I wish to seduce it to my viewpoint in the course of a sensual, mutual dance.

I've changed from a fox to a hedgehog. Taking Isaiah Berlin's famous metaphor, the fox knows many things and does them fluently, while the hedgehog knows one thing and stubbornly works till he does it to perfection. I can't claim to full hedgehog status yet, but I find that over the course of my creative life, a slightly scattershot approach to pieces, investigating a variety of aesthetics, styles and techniques, has yielded a series of discoveries and knowledge. These in turn have become increasingly merged into a single practice that continues to develop, and hopefully will continue to do so until my end. This is what I now will propose in the section that follows. The key to it all is how the idea of space I mentioned earlier found its fullest realization in my emerging conception of harmony.

2 Harmony as nature/Nature as harmony

In my mid-forties, I felt that my apprenticeship was finally drawing to a close. And that meant I needed to discover and embrace a more comprehensive and organic paradigm for my music, something more than the forays into a series of "etudes" that had given me experience and confidence, had successfully encountered a series of styles (both historical and "non-classical") and techniques, but had not yet knit together the different strands I'd investigated. I felt that my work needed a grounding in a *practice.* And by that I mean not just technique, but an overall aesthetic and conceptual framework from which grew a particular technique (and the technique as it grew would in turn inflect the framework). From 1998 to 2000 I wrote three works: *Open* for string trio, my second string quartet "*Fear of Death/Love of Life*," and the concluding movement of my Third Symphony, "*The World Turned Upside Down*." In these I began to see the outlines of a new practice based on a personal understanding of harmony, something that seemed natural and evident to my intellect and my ear.

Let me pull back for a moment. Earlier I'd spoken of how *space* as a concept and metaphor motivated my music. But the way I evoked it still remained a bit too "symbolic" for me, often denoted by extremes of register, expansive melodies, and a deeply breathing time-sense. What I felt I needed was to go to the point where the musical "space" I created was not represented by certain "external" characteristics, but evident instead by its capacity to *hold a maximum of information*. In short, if I could write music of greater richness and density, but that would still not feel crowded, clotted, or muddy, then that would be the proof of such space, and it would not need to be proclaimed. It would simply *exist*.

And the key to enlarging this space was harmony. I fully admit that while I've always felt I had a strong and clear harmonic sense, during my education I felt woefully inadequate when confronting common practice harmonic dictation. In college I was hapless with it. (Cage's story of his confrontation with Schoenberg over the issue had great resonance with me when I finally read it.) I could never intuitively analyze the chords I was hearing fast enough to label them with the Roman numerals. If I had been asked to sing an arpeggiation of the next logical chord in a sequence, I could have done that. But to hear it in the seeming fog of sound coming from a piano was barely possible for me. I think that one reason I was drawn to more atonal music was not that it was "easier" or that pitch "didn't matter," but rather that there I could just *use my ear* in the most direct and painstaking way possible.

But I also knew that wasn't enough. And so what seemed to emerge over time was a realization that *in the actual structure of sound itself* there was a model for harmonic practice, and that was the overtone series.

This is of course not new, and anyone who has read the preceding will have been well briefed about the issue in Chapter 4. My approach, while it has similarities to French spectralism (which I first encountered in 1980–81, the year I was a fellowship student in Paris), is more rooted in the early-twentieth-century American version, especially as articulated by Henry Cowell in his *New Musical Resources*. Between his theoretical attempt to create a "unified field theory" of music, connecting pitch, rhythm, and color by the common denominator of frequency *and* what I heard in the music of Ives (a harmonic field that accepted the entire chromatic and more, yet remained somehow "grounded" in a recognizable tonality), I started to see a possible practice emerging.

I've already spoken about how in the twentieth-century harmony became often equated in post-tonal practice as being an exercise in vertical *consistency*, especially in the way intervals were manipulated via set theory (both theoretically, in the case of Forte, and creatively, as in Carter). I wanted however to find *resonance*, some approach that allowed the constituent sounds of a piece to interact sympathetically, and open up the music to a new dimension of scale, depth, and expression. In a sense, harmony became the bridge that connected my fascination with space and time to their actualization. It's not easy to describe, but the sense of an evermore ample space for sound, facilitated by a harmonic practice that was properly "resonant," allowed for a flow of time that was both directed and circular, perhaps best thought of as spiraling. It became big enough to be both teleological and non-teleological at once.

All of this was arrived at very gradually, piecemeal. The critical step was to arrange the twelve chromatic pitches in a vertical order that followed the overtone series as closely as possible (see the figure in Chapter 4). As this was still in equal temperament, it was of course "cheating." But what I discovered was that the *sound* of this arrangement was evocative enough of the series to create a distinctive, identifiable harmonic world, one that could recur from piece to piece. Its *freshness* didn't wear out on repetition.

I need to make an important point here that distinguishes my approach from some others. So much of what is called microtonality falls into two camps. On the one hand there are different equal subdivisions of the traditional twelve equal-tempered tones, such as quarter-tones. Some of these in turn provide a closer approximation of more "perfect" intervals as they actually occur in the series. And then there is tuning that privileges particular intervals in their purest form, such as just intonation's fifths and thirds.

In retrospect I realize I've never been deeply attracted to either—even though as we'll see near the end of this chapter the idea of *precise tuning* that is rooted in overtone relations *is* critically important for me. Rather, the *overtone series itself*, both as a metaphor and a concrete reality, is what I feel has been guiding me, and I have been exploring. On the one hand, naïve as it is, it has felt to me like a gate into a more "natural" sound and flow of musical phenomena. And time after time, almost every risk I have taken, allowing "systematic" choices based on it to guide my writing, has given results that both surprised and delighted my ear. For the first time I have felt I've had a way to arrange previously overwhelming densities of notes (both in speed and simultaneity) in a manner that I could trust, even if I could not immediately predict the exact sound before it was executed. And at the same time, through this exploration my ear has been "trained" to hear and anticipate these results, so that they *have* become increasingly intuitive and internally heard.

The first piece where I felt I found a more comprehensive harmonic practice based on these principles was a short work for oboe, cello, and piano composed in June 2001 at Yaddo (and commissioned by the German ensemble PianOVo), *Coloring Sound's Scent.* Its key technical device was to create several of these "12-tone overtone rows" in advance on different fundamentals; then, after identifying common partials between them, using those as "pivots" to modulate from one series to another. Below is an example of this sort of harmonic shift (in this case, the fifth partial (G#) off a E fundamental becoming the nineteenth partial (Ab) off a F fundamental).

The next work that elaborated on this discovery was a short piano piece, *From the Ground Up.* Most of it was written on a plane trip I took in 2002 from Hartford to Minneapolis, and the fact that I could compose it without any aid

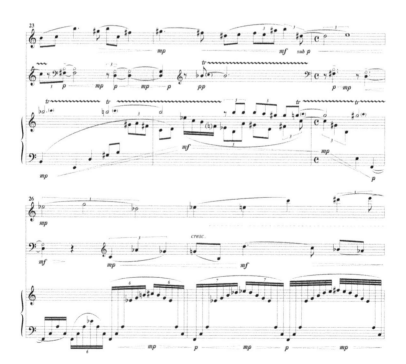

Example 9.1 *Coloring Sound's Scent,* mm.23–27.

except this set of constraints and my ear was liberating. The piece is written on three staves. In the middle one I composed a free, chant-like melody, fully intuitive. Then, taking that line as a starting point, I chose a series of notes within it to interpret as overtones off a particular fundamental. The notes of the line would thus be a "trigger" for an overtone-based texture that surrounded it; then the next successive set in this "cantus" would designate a new fundamental and respective partials within its series. In the opening of the piece, the mid-range D is first interpreted as a fifth partial of a Bb fundamental, then as the eleventh of Ab, and finally the third of G (the grace notes also help to define the fundamental by referencing the respective collection of partials).

At this point it was becoming clear that a more comprehensive view of the harmonic field in which I was playing could be defined. And this led to a third work, this one in fact an open-form improvisation, titled *Changing My Spots* (2005). It is a single-page score, showing six harmonic regions, each based on the same overtone-row structure, but off a different fundamental. Any group of players improvises on those pitches (in those registers) until cued to

Example 9.2 *From the Ground Up*, mm.1–13.

move to another region by a conductor or a designated player. The modulation is again effected by emphasis on common partials, which are now indicated in the score by connecting horizontal lines (and slurs). In addition, the six fundamentals of the respective regions are themselves the first six partials off the A fundamental (and as a serendipitous result, the whole collection of the six regions' pitches in fact defines the exact range from the lowest to the highest note of the piano keyboard).

This finally gave me a template to which I could return successively, a reference for harmonic relations and practice. Somewhat like Ives's experimental etudes, short works that allowed him to refine many radical aspects of his technique, yet which still had distinct aesthetic worth and profile, these three little pieces became a resource that allowed much larger pieces to emerge and which gave me confidence to pursue this course based on what I felt was their success (i.e., I loved the way they *sounded*).

At this point larger pieces now emerged. Two in particular presented a bolder face, *The Wind's Trace Rests on Leaves and Waves* for string quintet and *Shake the Tree* for piano four-hands,[5] both from 2005. The two principles guiding the pieces that were extensions of my initial discoveries were (1) moving through a series of harmonic regions in a predetermined order, usually arriving by the conclusion at the "tonic" fundamental from which the other regions' fundamentals were derived; and (2) creating a plan for sectional durations and tempi that was based on proportions from the Fibonacci series. Soon thereafter, these principles found what I felt to be their fullest realization in my fourth Symphony, "*The Ladder.*"

In moving to the orchestral realm, it became possible for the first time to present gestures that encompassed the entire harmonic field. For example, this passage near

Example 9.3 *Changing My Spots.*

Example 9.4 *Symphony No. 4*, mm. 49–57.

the opening encompasses the entire A-based, "overtone-row" (which opens the piece) in the strings, with the first appearance of the next related region, based on E (third partial of A) in the winds and brass. The percussion is by this point playing rhythms whose subdivisions approximately mirror the ratios of the harmonic series.

And this enlarged field of play *also* allowed for subsets of these vertical rows to be extracted and regrouped into a kaleidoscope of different harmonic forms. For example, in this example near the end of the first movement, using the vertical row now based on Eb, celesta, glockenspiel, vibraphone, and crotales are grouped into an "angelic choir" (shades of *Mathis*) each based on a different triad derived from the natural registration of its pitches in that harmonic matrix: respectively, Db minor, Ab augmented, Eb augmented, and D major.

Such events needed some sort of overarching structure to control their pacing and direction, and in this case I returned to the template of *Changing My Spots*. The major addition to this was the schemes for determining the sequence of the regions, and their relative durational proportions (see Figure 9.1). The work is in five movements, Moderato (though with a variety of internal changing tempi)-Fast-Slow-Fast-Moderato. Following the decreasing values of the Fibonacci series (starting from 8) the proportional size of each movement decreases (in actual duration). Each movement has six subsections (which accordingly grow shorter and shorter in the overall "squeeze"), each based on one of the six initial harmonic regions. This succession of these regions is systematic but basically intuitive; these shifts emerged in the sketching of the overall form, guided very much by taste and ear. Once established, though, these subsections' durations were governed by a strict proportion-game, that is, there is the same five-value descending Fibonacci sequence, but since there are six harmonic regions in each movement, their relation to the duration-proportions becomes an isorhythm. Finally, in the schema, the base unit in seconds for the proportion-value "1" in each subunit is given (note they also follow the Fibonacci series, with slight adjustments that came out of the final tweaking of the work), and their exact time-values are displayed on the bottom row of the chart.

By creating this architecture I took a principle I'd used in earlier pieces and moved it to a new level. And that is to *make a large piece out of many small ones.* By breaking down the sequence of sections, to the second, I now had a series of "molds" into which I could pour content, whose basic harmonic content I also already knew. With that background information defined, the act of composing in the moment felt liberated, and far more improvisational. I'd created my own "changes." As the piece was broken into a series of discrete creative steps, once

Example 9.5 *Symphony No.4*, mm. 183–198.

Movement:	**1**						**2**						**3**						**4**						**5**					
<u>Harmonic regions:</u>	[1	2	5	4	3	6|	[3	1	2	4	5	6|	[2	1	5	4	3	6|	[4	3	2	1	5	6|	[1	2	3	4	5	6|
<u>"Macro" Proportions:</u>	8						5						3						2						1					
<u>Actual Movement Timings:</u>	9'						5'32"						2'56"						1'45"						1'20"					
<u>Sub-Proportions:</u>	[8	5	3	2	1	8|	[5	3	2	1	8	5|	[1	8	5	3	2	1|	[8	5	3	2	1	2|	[1	2	3	4	5	6|
<u>Sub-unit Duration:</u>	21"(20)						13"						8"						5"						3"(2.5)					
<u>Actual Duration:</u>	[2'40"	1'40"	1'	40"	20"	40"]	[1'15"	39"	26"	13"	1'44"	1'15"]	[24"	16"	8"	1'04"	40"	24"]	[10"	5"	40"	25"	15"	10"]	[5"	10"]	3"	6"	9"	15"	24"	39"]

Harmonic and Temporal Structure of Symphony No.4

Figure 9.1 Temporal-Harmonic Structure of Symphony No.4.

each was finished, one moved on to the next with a sense of completion, no matter where in the course of the piece. I also found myself surprised that this sort of thinking had emerged in my practice. It is definitely what I would associate more with a composer like Elliott Carter (in terms of "macro-planning") and even Schoenberg (these *were* rows after all, albeit vertical, but still ordered by register). The irony was not lost on me, but from the outset my interest in Ives and Ruggles showed a taste for a sort of "transcendental architecture" in the music that moved me, so I shouldn't have been too surprised.

One other byproduct of this process was that finally I felt *I could write enough notes*. This sounds suspiciously like the emperor in *Amadeus* (albeit in reverse), but I'm not joking. If one deals with "notes & rhythms," a composer is always trying to string together discrete sonic events, each one supplanted by the next, though because of instruments' attack characteristics, many are "dying" from the moment they are sounded. As a result, it's critical to create the *illusion of continuity* in a work, a sense that a line or gesture is seamless. There are places for austerity and space, but other moments demand a beautiful excess. Now I knew that I could employ the overarching harmonic schema from which the pitches of a section emerged, with far less fear of a mistake or contradiction of meaning. Because the large-scale relations already sounded right to me, I could be confident that their local realizations would too.

A reader might be noting this emphasis on harmony and wondering if I have thought at all about rhythm. The answer is yes, but not as systematically. As my capacity to write genuine fast music has increased, so has my ability to take a plethora or notes, almost like air molecules, and shape them into wind, varying in direction, intensity, and pattern. And the proportion games I've outlined are themselves a sort of "macro-" or formal rhythm. On the largest scale the music now has a distinct pacing that drives long-range transitions and contrasts. And the Cowellian concept of a harmonic/timbral/rhythmic unity also influenced rhythmic choices and strategies on the local level. For example, I've found it increasingly convenient and stimulating to devise rhythmic ostinati of beat patterns themselves fashioned from Fibonacci sequences of durations; these can be very "groovy" yet asymmetric, regular yet not entirely predictable.

Over time, in the pursuit of increasing levels of harmonic hierarchy, I've extended the concept of the "overtone-row" to accommodate multiple and simultaneous versions thereof, serving different structural functions. By the time of my *Rocking Chair Serenade* (2013), I had developed a capacity to superimpose

Figure 9.2 Harmonic/Modal Structure, *Rocking Chair Serenade*.

these series, one derived from another. Take the following example from the piece, represented by the schematic in Figure 9.2.

The lowest staff (labeled "Master Mode") is the series that governs the entire piece. (Whole notes indicate pitch classes in their first appearance in the register closest to their overtone analogue; black noteheads represent these pitches as they continue to appear in octave doubling up the harmonic series. These notes can be used but ideally they should serve a more ornamental, less "structural" function.) The work's successive variations are in fact based on the partials Bb, D, E, F#, G, Ab, B, and C (eight of the twelve possible, and radiating out wedge-like from the middle). At the opening, Bb is explored in two ways: first, using the notes from the master mode starting from the Bb in its given register and second from top line. (In the example that follows, this constitutes the opening statement of the theme in unison, with selective coloristic doublings.) Then, starting at m.17 (labeled "Pre-Variation"), in higher register notes a line emerges that is derived from a new mode on Bb, following the same structure as that of the "master" C-based mode (top line of chart). Thus, two different interpretations of "harmonic Bb" can coexist, the latter serving an embellishing function.

One of the things that first drew me to this idea of harmony was its capacity to include the total chromatic whenever I wanted, yet also to retain a sense of spaciousness and order I've always valued from tonality. In my generation (one of the first "postmodern," in that the serialism/experimentalism/minimalism schisms and wars were already more or less passed by the time I/we attained

Example 9.6 *Rocking Chair Serenade*, mm. 1–15.

artistic maturity) a sort of Holy Grail was often posited as the capacity to blend atonality and tonality fluidly and effortlessly. This was laudable, and the plurality of it was exciting. But it still didn't seem enough to me; as I've remarked earlier, the juxtapositions and blends seemed more a matter of symbol than actual seamless substance. I'd always been drawn to the craggy Transcendentalist ethos of Ruggles, but despite an ironclad consistency, I found the music also abrasive in its ever-dissonant surface. I yearned for something that had its complexity yet also a certain purity. This emerged in my own work—once voicings based on overtone series became my primary material. In this sense I think I was modeling Ives more than Ruggles. And the tonal elements, in their purity, were to me "cleaner" than those of late-nineteenth-century chromatic harmony (though I'll always admit that Brahms seems able to achieve this sort of fullness, even voluptuousness of sound while never sacrificing clarity and directness, something that continues to awe me). Perhaps it was the fact that more consonant intervals were concentrated in lower register, suggesting a triadic grounding

Example 9.7 *Rocking Chair Serenade*, mm.16–22.

even if those triads moved in directions that had little or nothing to do with common practice functionality. In short, my "multimodal" emerging practice was another way to extend the range of a chromatic richness that didn't threaten to crowd or clot the spaciousness of the sound.[6]

This takes me up almost to the present moment of this writing. But all along, I've recognized that I've been "cheating" in one sense. Despite basing the entire harmonic armature on the overtone series, I'd continued to use equal temperament as the medium to realize it. For many this is a hopeless contradiction, one that undermines the very foundation of the practice and leaves it a house built on sand. I can't argue too much against this charge . . . *except* to say the following:

1) The world of sounds I've teased out is deeply satisfying for me. And similar constructs seem to be at work in a variety of composers who were sensitive to this viewpoint, again Ives and Debussy, two whom I revere. I do feel that freshness doesn't *have* to be in alternative intonation.

2) My friend Ingram Marshall once commented that perhaps the precision of the tuning didn't matter that much in my work, because what registered was that the sounds represented the harmonic series closely enough that the metaphor became a sort of reality. This falls into the category of what I've already called "close enough for rock & roll," which isn't as flippant as it first sounds.

3) A freedom to mix different intonational strategies, to use equal temperament when it is most useful and efficient, and other tunings when most appropriate, seems an increasing strategy of many composers. For me the greatest example and confirmation comes in the late works of Ligeti, such as the Violin and Horn Concertos.

4) Finally, I've noted an interesting acoustic/psychological phenomenon. When players are presented with these harmonic fields and progressions, within the limits of their instruments, they tend unconsciously to read toward a purer, overtone-based tuning.

These factors have reassured me that I'm not too far off from a viable course. But still . . . I've had an essential *curiosity* about how this world would sound in more precise tuning. And that term, "precise tuning" (which I first heard from John Luther Adams), seems very accurate and well, precise. It suggests a technique that can be driven by different ideals, systems, motivations. In my case it is to explore a greater purity of simultaneous sounds in the moment, but also to still have the possibility of *modulation* between different fields over the long haul. The present instant of the piece at any point can be perfected, but the pleasures of teleology not completely suppressed.

And so I've begun to work in a world of extended intonation. The first two pieces along these lines have been *Updraft* (2009) for ten trombones, and *Night Garden* (2013) for five contrabasses. Both exploit unique properties of the instrument—things players already know in their regular practice—to reach the harmonic goal.

Updraft's technique is based on the idea that in a single position a trombone can produce a harmonic series via embouchure alone, based on the fundamental of that position. So each trombone is in a fixed position at any given moment, though from one section to another they can change. Tenor trombones play from positions I, IV, and VII, with respective fundamentals of Bb, G, and E. Altos play in position II, with fundamental D. Basses play in position IX, with fundamental C. It is clear that these fundamentals in turn outline the first six different pitch classes to emerge as harmonics off a C fundamental. In addition, these fundamentals for each section are underlined by a drone modeled on the trombone, generated live by Max from laptop. The following excerpt shows two such transitions, with the drone shifting from G to E, and then to D.

There is also a formal and contrapuntal dance at work throughout, in that the opening unison line of the piece is stated in the next section at the transposition level of the new drone, and another line is added. *Then* the process is repeated in the following section with another transposition and line addition. As a result, the music becomes increasingly polyphonic and yet always retains a connection throughout of recurrent material. Additionally, each section's duration is expanded or contracted by the ratio of the two adjacent drones' interval, with the result that the music breathes more broadly the closer it is to its "home"

Example 9.8 *Updraft*, mm. 20–40.

partial of C. I don't think I've written another work with all its elements so strictly determined; I joke this is my "Ockeghem piece."

And one thing that also occurs in the course of the work is that due to the different frequencies that result from the ratios off different fundamentals, notes whose spelling in the score are enharmonically the same can become quite different in reality. Rather than disorienting I find this in fact thrilling; it is as though every pitch, not just pitch-class, has a unique color that renders the often dense texture still translucent. One hears the notes almost as individual planets flashing, vanishing, and returning in their own cosmic cycles.

Night Garden (2013) works from a similar principle of exploiting an instrument's idiomatic strengths. In this case it is the contrabass's capacity to sound strong natural harmonics higher up the series than other strings. Thus, the piece identifies the natural harmonics of the 2nd, 3rd, 4th 5th, 6th, and 7th on the C, E, A, D, and G strings; each instrument plays a different and only one of these strings throughout the piece (the low C comes from either a C extension or a five-string bass). Figure 9.3 shows the available pitches.

The result is a harmony that is more like a mist. The essential breathiness of the harmonics on the bass, combined with their strength, creates a sound that

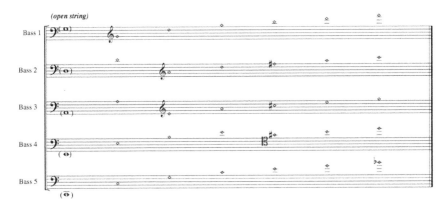

Figure 9.3 *Night Garden Harmonic Assignments.*

Example 9.9 *Night Garden*, mm.1–6.

Example 9.10 *Night Garden*, mm.72–80.

is clearly "tonal." Yet to me it also makes a sound that is on the porous threshold between harmony and color.

And despite this seeming straitjacket of constrictions, I find it liberating, allowing not only such homophonic passages as above, but highly contrapuntal ones, such as the following, which starting at m.75 is a strict five-part mensuration canon.

And this brings us close to the present. My third piano sonata, "Clouds of Clarification," ties together precise tuning with my previous harmonic practice. At first glance this seems contradictory, considering the piano as medium, but the key is the performance system of Aron Kallay, whose digital piano using Pianoteq software allows for instantaneous retuning of all eighty-eight keys to any frequency conceivable (the trick is that the sounds are resynthesized, rather than sampled). For me, this is a dream realized, and I have gone back and

REGION

One

	A	A#	B	C	C#	D	D#	E	F	F#	G	G#
RATIO	#1/1	17/16	#9/8	19/16	#5/4	21/16	#11/8	#3/2	13/8	27/16	#7/4	15/8
INTERVAL	1	1.0625	1.125	1.1875	1.25	1.3125	1.375	1.5	1.625	1.6875	1.75	1.875
CENTS	0	4	3	-1	-14	-30	-49	1	40	5	-32	-12

Two

	A	A#	B	C	C#	D	D#	E	F	F#	G	G#
RATIO	63/48	33/24	#9/6	39/24	81/48	21/12	45/24	#3/3	51/48	27/24	57/48	15/12
INTERVAL	1.3125	1.375	1.5	1.625	1.6875	1.75	1.875	1	1.0625	1.125	1.1875	1.25
INTERVAL	0.9844	1.03125	1.125	1.2188	1.2656	1.3125	1.4063	1.5	1.5938	1.6875	1.7813	1.875
CENTS	-28	-47	3	44	8	-30	-10	1	7	5	-1	-12

Three

	A	A#	B	C	C#	D	D#	E	F	F#	G	G#
RATIO	65/40	135/80	35/20	75/40	#5/5	85/80	45/40	95/80	25/20	105/80	55/40	15/10
INTERVAL	1.625	1.688	1.75	1.875	1	1.0625	1.125	1.1875	1.25	1.3125	1.375	1.5
INTERVAL	1.0156	1.05469	1.0938	1.1719	1.25	1.3281	1.4063	1.4844	1.5625	1.6406	1.7188	1.875
CENTS	26	-8	-45	-24	-14	-9	-10	-17	-28	-43	-63	-12

Four

	A	A#	B	C	C#	D	D#	E	F	F#	G	G#
RATIO	63/56	133/112	35/28	147/112	77/56	21/14	91/56	189/112	49/28	105/56	#7/7	119/112
INTERVAL	1.125	1.1875	1.25	1.3125	1.375	1.5	1.625	1.688	1.75	1.875	1	1.0625
INTERVAL	0.9844	1.03906	1.0938	1.1484	1.2031	1.3125	1.4219	1.4766	1.5313	1.6406	1.75	1.8594
CENTS	-28	-34	-45	-59	-80	-30	9	-26	-63	-43	-32	-27

Five

	A	A#	B	C	C#	D	D#	E	F	F#	G	G#
RATIO	63/36	135/72	#9/9	153/144	81/72	171/144	45/36	189/144	99/72	27/18	117/72	243/144
INTERVAL	1.75	1.875	1	1.0625	1.125	1.1875	1.25	1.3125	1.375	1.5	1.625	1.688
INTERVAL	1.0547	1.055	1.125	1.1953	1.2656	1.3359	1.4063	1.4766	1.5469	1.6875	1.8281	1.8984
CENTS	92	-8	3	11	8	1	-10	-26	-45	5	44	9

Six

	A	A#	B	C	C#	D	D#	E	F	F#	G	G#
RATIO	121/88	33/22	143/88	297/176	77/44	165/88	#11/11	187/176	99/88	209/176	55/44	231/176
INTERVAL	1.375	1.5	1.625	1.688	1.75	1.875	1	1.0625	1.125	1.1875	1.25	1.3125
INTERVAL	0.9453	1.03125	1.1172	1.1602	1.2031	1.2891	1.375	1.4609	1.5469	1.6328	1.7188	1.8047
CENTS	-98	-47	-9	-41	-80	-61	-49	-44	-45	-52	-63	-78

Figure 9.4 Tuning chart for *Piano Sonata No. 3, "Clouds of Clarification."*

written a work based on the same six-region harmonic schema that I devised in *Changing My Spots*. The difference is that now the pitches are all tuned to fall into the precise tunings that emerge from their true position in the overtone series. With the assistance of my former student and current colleague Matt Sargent, I now have the following translation of the system into non-equal-tempered frequencies.

(The information here should be clear to most of those who have followed my argument to this point, but I'll add that for regions 2–6, the two rows marked "Interval" are upper, the ratio governing tuning within the region itself, and lower, the ratio of tuning in relation to a "meta-fundamental" of A.)

And most recently (2015–present) I have been developing a piece in multiple iterations titled *Infinity Avenue*. In this, the original template of

Changing My Spots has been turned into a Max patch, where each of the six harmonic regions is now a set of pitches (realized via granular synthesis) justly tuned to exact overtones off each's fundamental. These then are played through in a random order, but without repeats until all twelve been played (things are becoming ever closer to serialism!). But they can be overlapped and superimposed, so as to create a vast polyphony if desired. I have performed this work as a solo laptop piece, and as an installation that goes for hours (either automatically or with my choosing and shaping the sonic "waves"). It has now become a work for an improvising ensemble of open instrumentation, the members of which respond to the electronic source. What I have learned from this is moving into a more "fixed" version for chamber orchestra that will by my Symphony No.7.

By my count, since *Coloring Sound's Scent* in 2001, I have written fifty-seven works that are grounded in this practice. They seem all "of a piece," and yet they vary greatly in tone, instrumentation, scale. One of the things I've discovered in the past fifteen or so years is that the act of composing has become a process of discovery with each piece. Before it was more a matter of extracting the work from myself, often a rough and demanding process. Now it feels more like performance itself, and if not certainly in real time, it does feel like an act of *play*. I feel I now enter into a musical field that is rich in harvestable sonic fruits. Using the tools I've developed, I'm able to "shake the tree" and harvest them.

In making this brief introduction to my practice, I've chosen pieces that tend to lend themselves more to detailed technical explanation and that reveal strict strategies and processes upon analysis. While this exposition gives a sense of how I approach the composition of almost every piece now, the degree of control and advance planning continues to vary. That very flexibility is part of the charm of the approach. I feel a grounding and simultaneous freedom by which I can choose how much I want to determine a piece's character and content in advance . . . or not.

And I'll end by saying that as soon as it starts to seem formulaic, I'll need to invent anew.

Postscript as Poem

Music is a vast space, endless, ever expanding.

Within it sounds begin to resonate, they take on life, both as individuals and as communities. They stir one another into movement, they dance, they shiver, they pause, they pray.

The sounds multiply, they become more numerous than their separate selves.

Silences also multiply and resonate. They become as varied as the sounds.

When listeners enter this space, they become amplified as well. They discover a capacity for greater breath, movement, and freedom than previously imagined.

I want to be the guide in that space.

At the end of a piece, I wish that the audience will have levitated. We'd need assistants to pull them from the ceiling, like balloons.

(Hartford, November 2019)

Notes

Preface

1   Indeed, while it will be footnoted, they will be mostly asides or directions to recordings of cited works . . . rather like this meta-footnote.

Chapter 1

1   Though one of the most electrifying musical experiences I had in my youth was Robert Shaw's performance of Ives's Second Orchestral Set, where he had the audience rehearse and then sing the *Te Deum* at the beginning of *In Hanover Square at the End of Tragic Day, the Voice of the People Again Arose.* I've never heard any concert again the same way after that.

2   Elllington 1943, from Carnegie Hall premiere recording, CD: Prestige #2PCD-304004-2; Mingus 1972, from Columbia album *Let My Children Hear Music* (reissue on Legacy SNYI 724172).

3   With one great exception, that is, in the American tradition many of these composers are co-equal with their lyricists, unlike European composers who set preexistent texts. So with those names let us also now enshrine Hart, Hammerstein, and Youmans.

4   And as proof from the current moment of the global impact, strange coagulant properties, and "soft power" of "Ameripop," take a look at the seemingly infinite series of music videos emerging worldwide as responses to Pharrell Williams's song "Happy": www.wearehappyfrom.com

5   Itself the title of his long-running blog.

6   The summer Lincoln Center series took note of this conundrum and turned it on itself, with the name "Serious Fun."

7   One particularly eye-opening book (for those not part of this scene) is John Seabrook's *The Song Machine: Inside the Hit Factory* (New York: Norton, 2015).

Chapter 2

1 Robert Carl, *Terry Riley's In C* (Oxford and New York: Oxford University Press, 2009).
2 CD recording of both *Mescalin Mix* and *The Gift:* Organ of Corti 1.
3 Stephen Wolfram, *A New Kind of Science* (Champaign: Wolfram Media, Inc., 2002).
4 CD recording: Nonesuch 759359-2.
5 At one of BOAC's annual Marathon concerts, a friend and eminent critic (Kyle Gann) came up to me and said, "It's over. Stravinsky won."
6 CD recordings: *Decasia* Canteloupe 21008; *Yo Shakespeare* Nonesuch 467708.
7 A point that was driven home to me (literally) during a two-day car ride along the western edge of the East Coast, watching the Appalachian landscape evolve as I listened to the Feldman Second.
8 CD Recording: Canteloupe 21072.
9 CD Recordings: *Roaratorio* Wergo 6303-2; *Ryonaji* Mode 41; the number pieces are so multitudinous it's hard to make any single recommendation, but an audio DVD disc of three orchestral works—108, 109, and 110—on CdBaby 5637722365 (by way of Ogre/Ogress) is impressive.
10 It's also revealing that they come after the long friendship and "mutual-mentorship" with Feldman. Cage's late "number pieces" show the younger composer's influence most directly in their sound and structure.
11 CD Recordings: *Strange and Sacred Noise* Mode 153; *Inuksuit* Cantaloupe 21096; *For Lou Harrison* New World 80669-2.
12 "Music as Place, Place as Music"; reprinted in *The Farthest Place: The Music of John Luther Adams*, ed. Bernd Herzogengrath (Boston: Northeastern University Press, 2012).
13 Finally, it is important to acknowledge one of the seminal texts of the last fifty years on the concept of musical time and its evolution, Jonathan Kramer's *The Time of Music* (New York and London: Schirmer, 1988).

Chapter 3

1 One of the rare instances of competing companies uniting for a universal standard for communication between their devices. It may be the most important "treaty" in the history of new music.
2 I am also seeing yet another variant beyond MIDI emerging in the composer's toolkit, that is works written in digital audio workstation (DAW) applications such as Logic. In this case, the piece one hears is the result of a series of soundfiles, arranged as tracks. They can be anything from live recordings to MIDI files, and

the result is increasingly a true "hybrid." And in fact it makes the language of the composer and the recording engineer evermore similar.

3   CD recordings: Varèse *Déserts, Ionisation, Hyperprism* London 289 640 208-2; Russolo historic recordings Sub Rosa 102-19; Gerhard Symphony No. 3, "Collages" Chandos 9556; Babbitt *Correspondences* BMOP Sound 1034; Cage *Imaginary Landscape No.4* Mode 229; Reich *Different Trains*, Nonesuch 79176-2, *City Life* Mode 214, *Three Tales*, Nonesuch 79662-2.

4   CD recording: Nonesuch 79249.

5   CD recordings: Adams Nonesuch 79360-2; Dresher New Albion 125.

6   CD recordings: Crumb Bridge 9139; Reich Nonesuch 79448.

7   CD recordings: Barlow Wergo 2010-50; Stone intone 10.

8   CD recordings: Teitelbaum New World 80756-2; Lewis Tzadik 8081.

Chapter 4

1   Arnold Schoenberg, *Harmonielehre* (Berekley and Los Angeles: University of California Press, 2010) (original printing 1911).

2   Lest I seem to tar postwar American serialists with too indiscriminately broad a brush, I'll add that there are several whose work still moves me: Donald Martino, George Perle, the early George Rochberg, and (still with us) Fred Lerdahl. Interestingly, each of these inflected traditional serial theory to create analogues to tonal practice. The results are as individualistic and varied as those of nineteenth-century composers, though of course with a far more chromatic palette.

3   While this will be elaborated in what follows, it's important to stress at the outset that this chart carries a basic compromise in showing sounding partials of given frequencies with a musical notation derived from equal temperament (ET). In fact, the seventh and eleventh partials are quite different from the notes indicated if they were played on a piano. Conversely, the "pure" third and sixth partials are slightly sharp in comparison to their ET versions. As a result, much of the microtonal literature avoids this discrepancy by speaking of the resultant pitches as a product of *ratios*, whose numerator and denominator are the positions of the partials within a common octave. Thus, for example, the seventh partial can be 7:4 (the latter being the appearance of the fundamental transposed to the octave register of the first appearance of the seventh partial).

Now all *this* truly opens up a wormhole that takes us down the rabbit hole! It is the subject of a very long book, but thankfully such is now available in Kyle Gann's *The Arithmetic of Listening: Tuning Theory for the Impractical Musician* (Urbana: University of Illinois Press, 2019) that is highly recommended to all.

4 Leonard Bernstein, *The Unanswered Question* (Cambridge: Harvard University Press), 1981.

5 Peter Burkholder, *All Made of Tunes: Charles Ives and the Uses of Musical Borrowing* (New Haven and London: Yale University Press, 1995), pp. 137–215.

6 CD recording: Sony 94731.

7 Jan Swafford, *Charles Ives: A Life with Music* (New York and London: W.W. Norton, 1995), p. 90.

8 I've found it possible to improvise a quick cartoon of an Ives piece at the piano. The recipe: in the bass, choose three tones and cycle through them, maybe a major triad or the scale degrees 1, 4, and 5; in the middle register, play unrelated, closed-position triads, major and minor; in the upper register make highly gestural splashes that use all twelve tones, though intuitively. Alternate and overlap between the three; the result will immediately evoke Ives, albeit a slapdash caricature.

9 CD recordings: *Housatonic at Stockbridge* and *From Hanover Square...* Naxos 8.559353, Symphony No.4 Sony 44939.

10 Henry Cowell, *New Musical Resources* (Cambridge, New York and Melbourne: Cambridge University Press, 1996) (original printing Alfred Knopf 1930).

11 For a more detailed description of the history of the book, Joel Sachs, *Henry Cowell: A Man Made of Music* (New York and Oxford: Oxford University Press, 2012), pp. 173–78.

12 Robert Carl, "Place and Space: The Vision of John Luther Adams in the Ultramodernist Tradition," in *The Farthest Place: The Music of John Luther Adams,* ed. Bernd Herzogengrath (Boston: Northeastern University Press, 2012), pp. 206–18.

13 Elliott Carter, *Harmony Book*, ed. Nicholas Hopkins and John Link (New York: Carl Fischer, 2002).

14 Olivier Messiaen, *The Technique of My Musical Language* (Paris: A. Leduc, 1956).

15 Indeed, what follows over the next few pages can now in retrospect perhaps be called the flowering of "classic postmodernism." Because of the often ironic commentary embodied in this music, it's "meta-quality," it stands out as different from the use of tonality by such composers as Bernstein, Rorem, Diamond, who saw themselves as the continuance of a grand tradition.

16 CD recordings: *Music for the Magic Theater* New World 80462; String Quartets No. 3-6 New World 80551-2; Rochberg's highly articulate exposition of his stance is represented by his essay collection *The Aesthetics of Survival*, ed. William Bolcom (Ann Arbor: University of Michigan Press, 1984).

17 CD recording: CRI 781.

18 CD recording: Decca 422.

19 CD recording: Erato 2292-45601-2.

20 CD recording: Naxos 8.559216-18.

21 Scelsi *Quatro Pezzi per orchestra* (1959); CD recording: Stradivarius 33803.

22 CD recording: Kairos 01422.

23 For a fascinating, if admittedly speculative, view of Debussy's music from this perspective, see: Roy Howat, *Debussy in Proportion: A Musical Analysis* (Cambridge, New York and Melbourne: Cambridge University Press, 1986).

24 Harry Partch, *Genesis of a Music* (New York: Da Capo Press, 1974).

25 CD recordings: String Quartets 2,3,4,9 New World 80637-2; String Quartets 1,5,10 New World 80693-2; String Quartets 6,7,8; New World 80730-2. Also, for detailed aesthetic and technical explanation, see the composer's collection of writings, *Maximum Clarity* (Urbana and Chicago: University of Illinois Press, 2006).

26 For a detailed description of Young's tuning for the piece, see: Kyle Gann, "La Monte Young's The Well-Tuned Piano," *Perspectives of New Music*, 31, no. 1 (Winter, 1993): 134–62. CD recordings: Young *The Well-Tuned Piano*, Grammavision B000009HZ9; Harrison *Revelation*, Cantaloupe 21043.

Chapter 5

1 For a comprehensive and insightful story of the piece, I recommend Kyle Gann's *No Such Thing as Silence: John Cage's 4'33"* (New Haven and London: Yale University Press, 2010).

2 It is important to note that the true *first* percussion pieces were written by the Cuban composer Amadeo Roldán, his fifth and sixth *Rítmicas*.

3 CD Recording: Works of the founders of the movement, Pierre Henry and Pierre Schaeffer (1953 and 1948, respectively), as well as Xenakis and Stockhausen, EI Records 159.

4 John Cage, "The Future of Music: Credo" (1939), from *Silence* (Middletown: Wesleyan University Press, 1961), pp. 3–6.

5 CD Recordings: Orchestral works ECM 461949-2; String Quartets Kairos 12662.

6 CD recordings: *Variations IV* Essential Media Group B003XF1S4G; *Child of Tree* Mode 272; *Score: Forty Drawings by Thoreau* does not seem to have any recording, even on YouTube. My memory comes from a performance in 1982 at New Music America Chicago.

7 It's also worth noting that artists tend to have very different tastes and expectations as an audience from those who regularly attend concerts. They have very little interest in virtuosity and may even be put off by it. The imagination put into the *presentation itself* may count as much as the product. It's no surprise then that the listeners that initially sustained the pioneering works of New York minimalism and experimentalism in the 1950 to the 1970s tended to come much more from the art rather than the music world.

8 And there is one example I mention that almost transcends this divide from the outset, that of R. Murray Shafer, the great Canadian composer, whose protean output contains cycles from string quartets to his Wagnerian-scale outdoor opera *Patria*. But though a composer, he has advocated (in a manner analogous to Oliveros) an intense listening and *structuring of the listening experience*, of the environment. This becomes a creative act for both artist and listener. His visionary text for this is *The Soundscape: Our Sonic Environment and the Tuning of the World* (Rochester: Destiny Books, 1977/1994).

9 John Luther Adams, *The Place Where You Go to Listen* (Middletown: Wesleyan University Press, 2009).

10 Janet Cardiff, *A Survey of Works*, with George Bures Miller (New York: P.S. 1 Contemporary Art Center, 2002) (to this date still the most comprehensive survey of the artist's work, though several of the pieces described in my text postdate it).

Chapter 6

1 CD recordings: Cage EMF Media B000NJM6VE; Brown Neos 11060; Boulez; Stockhausen Alga Marghen 54.

2 James Pritchett, *The Music of John Cage* (Cambridge, New York and Melbourne: Cambridge University Press, 1993), p. 126.

3 CD recording: Mode 112. Also cf. fn. 7, Ch. 3.

4 Pisaro's works are best explored through his own label, Gravity Waves. For a sample of Frey, see the collection of piano works performed by Andrew Lee on Irritable Hedgehog 006.

5 Iannis Xenakis, *Music and Architecture*, ed. and trans. Sharon Kanach (Hillsdale: Pendragon Press, 2008).

6 CD recording: Col Legno 20504. It's also interesting that the development of its large formal gestures was in fact driven by analysis of a sine wave pattern taking on more and more complexity, a function built into the composer's UPIC computer system. As such, this micro-to-macro process is related to the similar sonic research at the basis of classic spectral practice.

7 Exhibition catalogue: *Iannis Xenakis: Composer, Architect, Visionary* (New York: The Drawing Center, 2010).

8 CD recording, *La Legende D'Er*: Montaigne 782058. I heard the composer slyly remark at the International Computer Music Conference in Evanston, Illinois in 1978, "Here is a slide showing a drawing of the *Polytope*. Many people are going in . . . and only a few are coming out."

9 CD recording: New World 80712-2. This is part of a collection of works written for the Cunningham company over decades. New World also has an additional Tudor collection, 80737-2.

10 CD recording: Ambient Music 1: Music for Airports Astralworks B0002PZVH0 (1978).

11 And it's worth remembering that this approach containing all music within a unique fixed electroacoustic predates the digital revolution. *Musique Concrète* is at the classic example from the very beginning, and in the analog period of the 1960s, Morton Subotnick's album-length works such as *Silver Apples of the Moon* (1967) are definitive statements of an aesthetic where presentation was LP + Stereo + Listener = Concert.

12 CD recording: *United States* (1983), now only available as MP3 download.

13 CD Recording, *Atlas* ECM 437773, now only available as download; DVD, *Ellis Island/Book of Days* (available directly from meredithmonk.org).

14 I've also noted a recent development, that is an increasing number of female composer-singers. They tend to be more "classical" in their training and presentation, but they're also extremely adventurous in terms of genre-bending and extended techniques. I've mentioned this glancingly a few paragraphs back, but other examples are Susan Botti and Gilda Lyons. Kate Soper started her musical life as a singer-songwriter before discovering her current incarnation as a proponent of "philosophical theater/vaudeville." I can't help but feel that Monk's example has given a permission for these composers to partner their musicianship and imagination in fresh ways.

15 An interesting sort of political incorrectness.

16 George Russell, *The Lydian Chromatic Concept of Tonal Organization* (Brookline: Concept Publishing Co., 2008) (reprint of 1953 original).

17 As was the case with early-twentieth-century classical masterpieces, I don't think it is necessary to reference all the major earlier jazz masters listed here. But for the most recent ones cited, here are representative CD recordings: Moran *Modernistic* Blue Note 7 2435-39838-2; Coleman *Motherland Pulse* JMT 834 401-2; Schneider *Concert in the Garden* ArtShare 0001; Hersch *Let Yourself Go* Nonesuch79558-2; Caine *Goldberg Variations* Winter & Winter 910 054-2; Lewis already cited. Caine is an especially interesting case, as he is a classically trained composer/pianist (including study with George Rochberg) and a virtuosic jazzer. He is one of the few cases I can think of who takes works from the Western classical repertoire, and treats them as "standards," without a trace of condescension or treacly arrangement.

   And finally, we must note that the list of these "open-ended hybrid" composers just keeps growing. Vijay Iyer (pianist) and Tyshawn Sorey (drummer and trombonist) are just the latest examples to find a home in the highest institutions (Harvard and Wesleyan, respectively), while still gaining professional recognition in venues completely outside of academia.

18 CD recording: Tzadik 7335.

Chapter 7

1 YouTube: http://www.youtube.com/watch?v=GyceQFpSOjI.

2 Though after I wrote this, I have encountered *Music for Large Space*, by my late colleague David Macbride, which is one of the most simple, elegant, and ingenious incorporations of the audience as a continuous member into the entire work. YouTube: https://www.youtube.com/watch?v=Y87pyUREWXw.

3 YouTube: http://www.youtube.com/watch?v=4TFbRshiuC8.

4 Though not an example of literal videogame score composition, the composer Andrew Norman has written a wildly inventive "symphony-in-everything-but-name," *Play* (2013/16; BMOP/sound 1040), whose inspiration comes from the levels of difficulty in games.

5 CD Recording: Deutsche Grammophon 00289 477 7461.

   He has also garnered controversy with questions of how much of the final product of his works are due to the music of collaborators, and whether they have been sufficiently credited. It's a real question, though one that can also be applied to a historic master as Duke Ellington.

6 CD recording: Deutsche Grammophon 459 570-2.

7 CD recording: New World 80615-2.

8 Indeed, this idea of accepting the "enemy's" terms of engagement with subversive intent was achieved brilliantly by the Russian conceptual artists Komar and Melamid, in the work *People's Choice*. In it, using professional polling services, they were able to construct "most wanted" and "least wanted" paintings for a variety of countries. I suggest an internet search to see a few; they are revelatory about human nature and taste. And they extended the principle to music, in collaboration with the composer Dave Soldier (CD recording Dia 002). The result for my taste is too much of a joke to be as effective as the paintings. But the *idea* though is one for composers to remember; there may be ways to convert it yet into something far more culturally reverberant.

Chapter 8

1 One thinks of the epigram attributed to Mahler, "Tradition is not to preserve the ashes, but to pass on the flame."

2 DVD: Saariaho *Un Amour de Loin* (opera), Deutsche Grammophon B0004721-09; CD: Salonen *Violin Concerto* Deutsche Grammophon 001752102.

3 Though I have to say that some of Cage's pieces *are* resolutely immune to sonic beauty, especially some from the "middle" period of the highest degree of aleatorism and indeterminacy. But the astonishing, modally based "gamut" pieces up to 1950 and the flood of late "number" pieces show that despite a deep puritanical streak, Cage never lost his sensual instinct.

4 John Goodman, *Mingus Speaks* (Berkeley and Los Angeles: University of California Press, 2013), p. 53.

5 Indeed, in what follows some may feel that what I've proposing as the emerging common practice is in fact a "post-Ivesian" practice. They wouldn't be far off.

6 The range and the number of Ligeti works are such that I will not give recordings for all those cited here. But the complete works series begun by Sony (62305-62311) and completed by Teldec (83953-88261) gives access to the complete catalogue.

7 CD recording: Piano Classics 19 (Oppens).

8 Carl Dahlhaus, *The Idea of Absolute Music* (Chicago: University of Chicago Press, 1991), p. 18.

9 Indeed, I've joked that if silicone-based life forms eventually replace the current carbon-based ones, they may find the "Two B's"—Babbitt and Bach—to be the greatest of all composers.

10 Careful readers may at this point spot what might seem an inherent contradiction in my argument: How can I denigrate the precedence of the symbolic over the acoustic in my critique of modernist practice, and now say that "sounds can begin to take on roles and meanings that go beyond themselves"? If you ask this question, congratulations on your insight. But I *do* have an answer, and it has to do with the issue of scale. If such "symbolism" governs the level of the music that deals with the moment-to-moment flow of its aural surface, then there are problems. But if "extra-musical" elements inspire that sonic fabric and in turn emerge from it without diverting it too far from its inherent tendencies, I think we will have a most fruitful interchange between micro and macro.

11 Bill McKibben, *Eaarth: Making of Life on a Tough New Planet* (New York: Times Books/Henry Holt & Co., 2011).

12 And tied to that is the increasing *parity of viewing platforms*. It's true, a pop icon will get millions of views on YouTube, while Ligeti (or you) receive comparatively only a handful. But the fact remains that now all these aural artifacts are equally accessible and share the same presentation format. It creates a *reception spectrum* like we've never had before, and you stand as a point upon it in far more equality and autonomy than ever.

13 Brian Cook, personal communication to the author.

Chapter 9

1 This was driven home by a single epiphanic experience. Walking over the railroad bridge near Place De L'Europe one fine spring day, I saw a flower-merchant's sidewalk display. Every posy she exhibited was perfect in its arrangement of shape, color, density. At that moment I finally understood Debussy.

2 Virgil Thomson, "The State of Music" (1939/61), from *A Virgil Thomson Reader*, ed. Tim Page (Boston: Houghton Mifflin, 1981).

3 Stephen Mithen, *The Singing Neanderthals* (Cambridge: Harvard University Press, 2006).

4 Symphony No. 2.

5 Shake the Tree, Innova Recordings 857.

6 One exception to this approach was my chamber orchestra work *A Musical Enquiry into the Sublime and Beautiful* (2005). In this I based successive movements on vertical harmonic rows that followed the overtone series both up (in the "normal" fashion) and down ("undertone" rows). These were meant to represent the beautiful and the sublime, respectively, following Edmund Burke's taxonomy. These worked well for their purposes, but the problem emerged in my attempt to combine the two in the final movement, in search of transcendent synthesis. To my ear, the result was a sort of "phase cancellation" of the power of each by the other.

Bibliography

The following is a highly selective list of books that have been important to me throughout my musical life and which have contributed to the intellectual and aesthetic development of these chapters. Of course, every title mentioned in the text is included. But beyond that, I have added a wider set of works whose importance I find real and helpful to anyone who chooses to ponder and grapple with the issues I've raised. Some weren't mentioned in the text but are obviously a major part of the current critical discourse, such as Alex Ross's *The Rest Is Noise*. Some go much farther back into the twentieth century, but remain relevant to the issues raised here, such as Stravinsky and Schoenberg (even Rameau!). Some are sui generis feats of intellectual imagination, inspirational in the way they leap disciplinary boundaries (Adorno, Andriessen, Mithen, Rosen, and Meyer); others inspired revelations of "the way things work" (Thomson).

Rather than parse them out by subject and try to tie them to the chapters of this book, I've let them mix and marinate. While I admit it's something of a sideways self-portrait, I hope that those who explore it will discover a fruitful cross-pollination for themselves. (The list is completely idiosyncratic; if I tried to create a comprehensive bibliography of the literature that relates to my topic, it would be longer than the book itself.) So if you read any one of these, look at *its* bibliography to follow the links. From this you may find yourself building your own diverse, open, personal library of techniques and concepts.

Adams, John Luther, *The Place Where You Go to Listen*. Middletown: Wesleyan University Press, 2009.

Adorno, Theodore, *Philosophy of Modern Music*. New York: The Seabury Press, 1973.

Andriessen, Louis and Schönberger, Elmer. *The Apollonian Clockwork: On Stravinsky*. Amsterdam: Amsterdam University Press, 2006 (original printing 1989).

Babbitt, Milton, *Words About Music*, edited by Stephen Dembski and Joseph N. Strauss. Madison: University of Wisconsin Press, 1987.

Bernstein, Leonard, *The Unanswered Question*. Cambridge: Harvard University Press, 1981.

Brant, Henry, *Textures and Timbres: An Orchestrator's Handbook*. New York: Carl Fischer Music, 2009.

Budiansky, Stephen, *Mad Music: Charles Ives, the Nostalgic Rebel*. ForeEdge: University Press of New England (Lebanon), 2014.

Burkholder, Peter, *All Made of Tunes: Charles Ives and the Uses of Musical Borrowing*. New Haven and London: Yale University Press, 1995.

Cage, John, *Silence*. Middletown: Wesleyan University Press, 1961.

Cagne, Cole and Caras, Tracy, *Soundpieces: Interviews With American Composers*, Metuchen, New Jersey and London: Scarecrow Press, 1982.

Cardiff, Janet, *A Survey of Works, with George Bures Miller*. New York: P.S. 1 Contemporary Arts Center, 2002.

Carl, Robert, *Terry Riley's In C*. Oxford and New York: Oxford University Press, 2009.

Carter, Elliott, *The Writings of Elliott Carter*. Bloomington and London: University of Indiana Press, 1977.

Carter, Elliott, *Harmony Book*, edited by Nicholas Hopkins and John Link. New York: Carl Fisher, 2002.

Cheng, Will, *Sound Play: Video Games and the Musical Imagination*. Oxford and New York: Oxford University Press, 2014.

Cowell, Henry, *New Musical Resources*, edited by David Nichols. Cambridge and New York: Cambridge University Press, 1996 (original printing 1930).

Dahlhaus, Carl, *The Idea of Absolute Music*. Chicago: University of Chicago Press, 1991.

Duckworth, William, *Virtual Music: How the Web Got Wired for Sound*. New York: Routledge, 2005.

Feldman, Morton, *Give My Regards to Eighth Street*, edited by B. H. Friedman. Cambridge, Exact Change, 2004.

Fink, Robert, *Repeating Ourselves: American Minimal Music As Cultural Practice*. Berkeley and Los Angeles: University of California Press, 2005.

Gann, Kyle, *American Music in the Twentieth Century*. New York: Schirmer, 1997.

Gann, Kyle, *No Such Thing as Silence: John Cage's 4'33"*. New Haven and London: Yale University Press, 2010.

Gann, Kyle, *The Arithmetic of Listening: Tuning Theory for the Impractical Musician*. Urbana: University of Illinois Press, 2019.

Goodman, John, *Mingus Speaks*. Berkeley and Los Angeles: University of California Press, 2013.

Grant, Mark, *Maestros of the Pen: A History of Music Criticism in America*. Boston: Northeastern University Press, 1998.

Grimshaw, Jeremy, *Draw a Straight Line and Follow It: The Music and Mysticism of LaMonte Young*. Oxford and New York: Oxford University Press, 2011.

Herzogengrath, Bernd, ed., *The Farthest Place: The Music of John Luther Adams*. Boston: Northeastern University Press, 2012.

Iannis Xenakis: Composer, Architect, Visionary, [exhibition catalogue]. New York: The Drawing Center, 2010.

Ives, Charles, *Essays Before a Sonata, The Majority, and Other Writings*, edited by Howard Boatright. New York: W.W. Norton, 1962.

Johnston, Ben, *Maximum Clarity and other Writings on Music*, edited by Bob Gilmore. Urbana and Chicago: University of Illinois Press, 2006.

Kim-Cohen, Seth, *In the Blink of An Ear: Towards a Non-Cochlear Sonic Art*. New York: Bloomsbury Academic, 2009.

Kramer, Jonathan, *The Time of Music*. New York and London: Schirmer, 1988 (currently out of print).

Kramer, Jonathan, *Postmodern Music, Postmodern Listening*, edited by Robert Carl. New York and London: Bloomsbury Academic, 2016.

Lewis, George E., *A Power Stronger Than Itself: The AACM and the American Experimental Tradition*. Chicago: University of Chicago Press, 2008.

McClary, Susan, *Feminine Endings: Music, Gender and Sexuality*. Minneapolis: University of Minnesota Press, 1991.

McKibben, Bill, *Earth: Making of Life on a Tough New Planet*. New York: Times Books/ Henry Holt & Co., 2011.

Messiaen, Olivier, *The Technique of My Musical Language*, translated by John Satterfield. Paris: Alphonse Leduc, 1956 (original printing 1944).

Meyer, Leonard, *Emotion and Meaning in Music*. Chicago: University of Chicago Press, 1956.

Mithen, Stephen, *The Singing Neanderthals: The Origins of Music, Language, Mind, and Body*. Cambridge: Harvard University Press, 2006.

Partch, Harry, *Genesis of a Music*. New York: Da Capo Press, 1974.

Potter, Keith, *Four American Minimalists: LaMonte Yong, Terry Riley, Steve Reich, and Philip Glass*. Cambridge and New York: Cambridge University Press, 2000.

Pritchett, James, *The Music of John Cage*. Cambridge, New York and Melbourne: Cambridge University Press, 1993.

Rameau, Jean-Philippe, *Treatise on Harmony*, translated by Philip Gossett. New York: Dover, 1971.

Reich, Steve, *Writings about Music, 1965–2000*. Oxford and New York: Oxford University Press, 2002.

Rochberg, George, *The Aesthetics of Survival*, ed. Bolcom, William. Ann Arbor: University of Michigan Press, 1984.

Rockwell, John, *All-American Music: Composition in the Late Twentieth Century*. New York: Alfred A Knopf, 1983 (currently out of print).

Rosen, Charles, *The Classical Style*. New York: W.W. Norton, 1998.

Ross, Alex, *The Rest Is Noise: Listening to the Twentieth Century*. New York: Farrar, Straus and Giroux, 2007.

Russell, George, *The Lydian Chromatic Concept of Tonal Organization*. Brookline, MA: Concept Publishing Co., 2008 (reprint of 1953 original).

Rutherford-Johnson, Tim, *Music After the Fall: Modern Composition Since 1989*. Oakland: University of California Press, 2017.

Seabrook, John, *The Song Machine: Inside the Hit Factory*. New York and London: W.W. Norton, 2015.

Schafer, R. Murray, *The Soundscape: Our Sonic Environment and the Tuning of the World*. Rochester: Destiny Books, 1977/1994.

Schoenberg, Arnold, *Harmonielehre*. Berkeley and Los Angeles: University of California Press, 2010 (original printing 1911).

Schoenberg, Arnold, *Style and Idea*, edited by Leonard Stein. Berkeley and Los Angeles: University of California Press, 2010 (original printing 1975).

Smith, Geoff and Walker, Nicola, *New Voices: American Composers Talk about Their Music*. Portland: Amadeus Press, 1995.

Steinetz, Richard, *György Ligeti: Music of the Imagination*. Boston: Northeastern University Press, 2003.

Stravinsky, Igor, *Poetics of Music*. Cambridge and London: Harvard University Press, 1975 (original printing 1942).

Strickland, Edward, *American Composers: Dialogues on Contemporary Music*. Bloomington and Indianapolis: Indiana University Press, 1991.

Swafford, Jan, *Charles Ives: A Life with Music*. New York and London: W.W. Norton, 1995.

Takemitsu, Toru, *Confronting Silence*. Berkeley: Fallen Leaf Press, 1995*.

Tenney, James, *From Scratch: Writings in Music Theory*, edited by Larry Polansky, Lauren Pratt, Robert Wannakaer and Winter Michael. Urbana, Chicago, and Springfield: University of Illinois Press, 2015.

Thomson, Virgil, *The State of Music and Other Writings*, edited by Tim Page. New York: Library of America, 2016 (original printing 1939/61).

Winkler, Todd, *Composing Interactive Music: Techniques and Ideas Using Max*. Cambridge: MIT University Press, 2001.

Wolfram, Stephen; *A New Kind of Science*. Champaign: Wolfram Media, Inc., 2002.

Xenakis, Iannis, *Music and Architecture*, edited and translated by Sharon Kanach. Hillsdale: Pendragon Press, 2008.

Index

www.ingramcontent.com/pod-product-compliance
Ingram Content Group UK Ltd.
Pitfield, Milton Keynes, MK11 3LW, UK
UKHW031251020325
455690UK00007B/112